TRANSPORTATION ISSUES, POLICIES AND R&D

CARGO PREFERENCES FOR U.S.-FLAG SHIPPING

BACKGROUND, CONSIDERATIONS, AND FOOD AID ISSUES

TRANSPORTATION ISSUES, POLICIES AND R&D

Additional books in this series can be found on Nova's website under the Series tab.

Additional e-books in this series can be found on Nova's website under the e-book tab.

TRANSPORTATION ISSUES, POLICIES AND R&D

CARGO PREFERENCES FOR U.S.-FLAG SHIPPING

BACKGROUND, CONSIDERATIONS, AND FOOD AID ISSUES

EDMUND SUTTON
EDITOR

NOVINKA

New York

NOTICE TO THE READER

The Publisher has taken reasonable care in the preparation of this book, but makes no expressed or implied warranty of any kind and assumes no responsibility for any errors or omissions. No liability is assumed for incidental or consequential damages in connection with or arising out of information contained in this book. The Publisher shall not be liable for any special, consequential, or exemplary damages resulting, in whole or in part, from the readers' use of, or reliance upon, this material. Any parts of this book based on government reports are so indicated and copyright is claimed for those parts to the extent applicable to compilations of such works.

Independent verification should be sought for any data, advice or recommendations contained in this book. In addition, no responsibility is assumed by the publisher for any injury and/or damage to persons or property arising from any methods, products, instructions, ideas or otherwise contained in this publication.

This publication is designed to provide accurate and authoritative information with regard to the subject matter covered herein. It is sold with the clear understanding that the Publisher is not engaged in rendering legal or any other professional services. If legal or any other expert assistance is required, the services of a competent person should be sought. FROM A DECLARATION OF PARTICIPANTS JOINTLY ADOPTED BY A COMMITTEE OF THE AMERICAN BAR ASSOCIATION AND A COMMITTEE OF PUBLISHERS.

Additional color graphics may be available in the e-book version of this book.

Library of Congress Cataloging-in-Publication Data

ISBN: 978-1-63484-945-6

Published by Nova Science Publishers, Inc. † New York

CONTENTS

PREFACE

Long-standing U.S. policy has treated the U.S.-flag international fleet as a naval auxiliary to be available in times of war or national emergency. When the United States is involved in an extended military conflict overseas, 90% or more of military cargoes are typically carried by ship. To support the U.S. merchant marine, Congress has required that "government-impelled" cargo sent overseas be carried on U.S.-flag ships. Government-impelled cargo (a.k.a. "preference cargo") is government-owned cargo, such as military supplies and food aid, and any cargo that is somehow financed by the federal government, such as by the Export-Import Bank. While export shipments account for the vast bulk of government-impelled cargo, in 2008 Congress extended the law to require that state and local governments and private entities importing goods with federal financial assistance ship at least 50% of such cargo in U.S.-flag vessels. Regulations to implement that requirement have not been issued. This book explains the motivation behind cargo preference law, discusses issues concerning the cost-effectiveness of the program, reviews attempts to apply cargo preference to the nation's oil trade, and identifies several disparate bills reflecting wide disagreement on the future direction of cargo preference policy. The book also examines cargo preference for food aid's (CPFA) impact on food aid shipping cost and U.S. agencies' implementation of CPFA requirements, and the extent to which the implementation of CPFA requirements contributes to sufficient sealift capacity.

In: Cargo Preferences for U.S.-Flag Shipping ISBN: 978-1-63484-945-6
Editor: Edmund Sutton

Chapter 1

CARGO PREFERENCES FOR U.S.-FLAG SHIPPING*

John Frittelli

SUMMARY

Long-standing U.S. policy has treated the U.S.-flag international fleet as a naval auxiliary to be available in times of war or national emergency. When the United States is involved in an extended military conflict overseas, 90% or more of military cargoes are typically carried by ship. To support the U.S. merchant marine, Congress has required that "government-impelled" cargo sent overseas be carried on U.S.-flag ships. Government-impelled cargo (a.k.a. "preference cargo") is government-owned cargo, such as military supplies and food aid, and any cargo that is somehow financed by the federal government, such as by the Export-Import Bank. While export shipments account for the vast bulk of government-impelled cargo, in 2008 Congress extended the law to require that state and local governments and private entities importing goods with federal financial assistance ship at least 50% of such cargo in U.S.-flag vessels. Regulations to implement that requirement have not been issued.

Historically, cargo preference law has been used to assure that a large proportion of government-impelled cargoes is shipped in *privately*

* This is an edited, reformatted and augmented version of a Congressional Research Service publication R44254, prepared for Members and Committees of Congress, dated October 29, 2015.

owned U.S.-flag ships rather than in *government*-owned vessels such as those now controlled by the Military Sealift Command (MSC). Military cargo then, and more so now, accounts for the overwhelming bulk of preference cargoes. Since 1954, an agreement between U.S. government cabinet departments has restricted the size of the military-owned fleet and has required the military to turn first to the private fleet before using its own ships. The cost of employing U.S. citizens aboard U.S.-flag commercial vessels appears to be higher than the costs of employing the federal civilian mariners that crew government-owned ships.

It appears preference cargo now accounts for almost all of the revenues of the U.S.-flag international fleet. U.S.-flag ships do not appear competitive with foreign-flag ships in carrying the overwhelming bulk of exports and imports transacted in the private sector. However, Congress has directed that the U.S. government pay the additional cost of U.S.-flag shipping in order to maintain the U.S.-flag international fleet as a naval auxiliary to be available in times of war or national emergency. This cost may be influenced by the level of competition among U.S.- flag carriers bidding for preference cargoes and the procedures for determining "fair and reasonable rates."

The needs of the commercial market increasingly have diverged from those of the military, as the trend toward highly specialized and larger ships in the commercial sector appears inconsistent with the military's shipping requirements. However, the knowledge and skills of the mariners aboard U.S.-flag commercial ships are transferrable to manning a military reserve fleet of ships.

In the 114th Congress, several disparate bills would have the effect of either increasing or decreasing the volume of preference cargo significantly. The bills involve the future of food-aid policy, the existence of the Export-Import Bank, and the level of operating subsidy provided to U.S.-flag carriers. The boom in domestic oil and gas production also has led to discussions in Congress about whether U.S.-flag tankers should be guaranteed a portion of the cargo if these products are exported. These issues are arising at a time when U.S.-flag operators face a potential decline in the amount of preference cargo due to overseas troop withdrawals and changes in food-aid policy.

INTRODUCTION

Long-standing U.S. policy has treated the U.S.-flag international fleet as a naval auxiliary to be available in times of war or national emergency. When the United States is involved in an extended military conflict overseas, 90% or more of military cargoes are typically carried by ship. Congress also has determined that for economic security reasons, the United States should have a commercial fleet active in international commerce.[1]

To support the U.S.-flag international fleet, Congress has required that "government-impelled" cargo sent overseas be carried on U.S.-flag ships. Government-impelled cargo is government-owned cargo such as military supplies, foreign aid such as food, and any privately owned cargo financed by the federal government, such as goods purchased with an Export-Import Bank loan. Regulations suggested, but not formally proposed, by the U.S. Maritime Administration (MARAD) would also require that some U.S.-bound cargo financed by the government be carried on U.S.-flag ships.[2] Cargo reserved for U.S.-flag vessels is referred to as "preference cargo."[3]

Cargo preference requirements are highly controversial, particularly among shippers of civilian aid cargoes, because they significantly increase shipping costs and may delay shipments.[4] However, preference cargo is critical to some U.S.-flag ship lines, as U.S.-flag ships are not price-competitive with foreign-flag ships in carrying the overwhelming bulk of exports and imports transacted in the private sector.

This report explains the motivation behind cargo preference law, discusses issues concerning the cost-effectiveness of the program, and reviews attempts to apply cargo preference to the nation's oil trade. The report also identifies several disparate bills reflecting wide disagreement on the future direction of cargo preference policy.

THE THREE U.S.-FLAG FLEETS

The United States has three separate U.S.-flag fleets capable of carrying commercial cargo.

The *U.S.-flag domestic fleet* comprises ships and barges that carry cargo and passengers between U.S. ports, including most U.S. island territories. Under a 1920 law, the Jones Act, such activity may be conducted only by vessels under U.S. ownership, built in the United States, and crewed by U.S. citizens.[5] The domestic fleet is often referred to as the "Jones Act" fleet.[6] These vessels do not receive direct government subsidies, but benefit by having exclusive access to cargoes such as oil shipments from Texas to the Northeast and goods moving by containership from California to Hawaii. Jones Act ships are not affected by cargo preferences, because the services they provide cannot be offered by foreign-flag ships.

The *U.S.-flag international fleet* comprises vessels registered under U.S. law that carry cargo and passengers between the United States and other countries. U.S.-flag ships in foreign trade must be owned and crewed by U.S. citizens,[7] but need not be built in the United States. Unlike the Jones Act fleet, the U.S.-flag international fleet faces competition from vessels registered in other countries. The privately owned U.S.-flag international cargo fleet consists of roughly 80 ships, including 43 containerships and 18 ships with roll-on/roll-off ramps to transport vehicles, including military vehicles.[8] The fleet is owned by 19 different ocean carriers and is crewed by a pool of approximately 3,200 private-sector merchant mariners.

The *Military Sealift Command* (MSC) in the Department of Defense (DOD) operates a fleet of about 120 ships. Many of these resupply Navy combatant ships at sea (an activity called "unrep," for underway replenishment) or perform missions such as ocean surveillance and submarine tendering. Approximately 50 MSC vessels carry military cargoes in port-to-port voyages similar to those undertaken by commercial ships. The cargo component of the MSC fleet includes oil tankers, containerships, and ships designed to carry oversize cargo, but the most prevalent type is roll-on/roll-off ships. The MSC fleet is mostly crewed by about 6,000 licensed mariners, who are federal civilian employees. The vessels these civilian mariners (known as "CivMars") crew do not plan to sail in combat waters. The MSC does not receive a direct appropriation from Congress. It bills DOD for the ocean transportation services it provides, and its budget is delineated in "working capital funds."[9]

The government-owned fleet of cargo ships also includes a reserve fleet of inactive vessels available for military deployment. These vessels are on standby at various ports. The Ready Reserve Force (RRF) consists of 46 ships that can sail upon either five or 10 days' notice. The RRF has a skeleton crew of 460 commercial mariners (10 per ship), but would require an additional 1,200 mariners to sustain its operation once activated.[10] The average age of the ships in the RRF is 40 years, about 20 years beyond the typical economic life of a foreign-flag commercial ship. The RRF consists mostly of roll-on/roll-off ships, and is a subset of a larger National Defense Reserve Fleet (NDRF), which also comprises vessels not expected to be activated on short notice and ships that are ready for scrapping. The NDRF is managed by MARAD, an agency of the U.S. Department of Transportation, in peacetime and the MSC when activated for military deployment. The reserve fleet is relevant to cargo preference because the U.S.-flag privately owned fleet provides employment for mariners who would be drawn upon to sail reserve fleet ships when activated.

The existence of both a privately owned deep-sea U.S.-flag fleet and a government-owned fleet capable of carrying similar types of military cargo overseas is a key motivation behind cargo preference laws.

A Brief History of the Cargo Preference Act of 1954

In the Military Transportation Act of 1904 (P.L. 58-198), Congress required that all U.S. military supplies be transported on U.S. vessels but did not specify whether government-owned or privately owned U.S.-flag vessels had to be used. In 1949, the Army's Transport Service, including 241 ships, was consolidated with the Navy's cargo (noncombatant) fleet of 94 ships to form the Military Sea Transportation Service (MSTS), with a total fleet of 335 ships.[11] The MSTS fleet carried not only strictly military personnel and cargo, but also significant amounts of military-related cargo such as the dependents and personal property of military personnel and employees of military contractors. Foreigners with government grants to study at U.S. universities, civilian employees of other federal agencies, and refugees and displaced persons also traveled aboard MSTS ships. Moreover, MSTS ships often sailed to and from busy ports that also were served by commercial carriers. The MSTS found that it could transport passengers and cargo in government-owned vessels for 80% or less of the cost of using private U.S.-flag shipping space.[12]

According to a 2004 study, the privately owned U.S.-flag carriers were not competitive vis-à-vis foreign-flag carriers in carrying commercial U.S. imports and exports after World War II, and therefore "lobbied strenuously for the military's business." They sought to limit the size of the MSTS fleet, fearing that its expansion could ultimately result in the nationalization of the U.S.- flag fleet. Carriage of military cargoes was also important for private U.S.-flag operators as a basis for claiming political support, as it allowed them to point to their role in providing sealift in wartime.[13] In a 1950 Senate hearing, the MSTS commander revealed that it was MSTS policy to maximize the use of its own ships before cargo was offered to commercial carriers.[14]

In 1951, the Department of Commerce, then the parent agency of MARAD, signed a memorandum of understanding with DOD identifying the priority MSTS was to follow in obtaining additional shipping capacity. First, it would purchase space on privately owned U.S.-flag liner[15] services; second, it would charter privately owned U.S.-flag vessels; third, it would activate government-owned vessels held in the military reserve fleet. Only after all those options were exhausted would MSTS buy space on or charter foreign-flag ships.[16] In 1954, the two departments signed another memorandum of understanding that severely restricted the size of the MSTS fleet to 151 ships and required approval of both secretaries for nonemergency expansion of the fleet. The objective of restricting the size of the MSTS fleet was to commit more military cargo to the privately owned U.S.-flag fleet. The "Wilson-Weeks" agreement, named after the two secretaries, remains substantively in effect today.[17]

Competition between the government-owned and privately owned fleets in carrying military-related cargo gave impetus to the Cargo Preference Act of 1954 (P.L. 83-644).[18] As originally introduced, the act would have eliminated the MSTS entirely, requiring that 100% of government-impelled cargoes be carried in *privately* owned U.S.-flag vessels. Due to opposition from the Eisenhower Administration, which favored repealing cargo preference requirements in favor of direct subsidies to U.S.-flag operators, the 100% requirement was reduced to 50%, the Commerce Department was relieved of direct responsibility for administering the law, and a provision was added requiring that U.S.-flag commercial vessels charge the government "fair and reasonable rates." The clear intent of the legislation was to encourage greater use of U.S.-flag private operators and reduce the role of the MSTS as a vessel operator.[19]

Since passage of the 1954 act, Congress has amended the Cargo Preference Act numerous times, generally in favor of private U.S.-flag carriers. U.S. foreign-aid cargo was a substantial share of total U.S. exports in the 1950s, and many of the amendments concerned carriage of food aid.

In 1961 (P.L. 87-266), Congress required that ships eligible for food-aid cargoes must either be built in the United States, or, if built abroad, must have sailed under the U.S. flag for the previous three years. Congress wanted to discourage foreign-flag ships from entering the U.S. cargo preference trade only temporarily in periods when the world shipping market was oversupplied. In the Merchant Marine Act of 1970 (P.L. 91-469), Congress empowered MARAD to regulate how other federal agencies should comply with the 1954 act after hearing allegations that other agencies intentionally did not fully comply with the law or interpreted the law differently than MARAD.[20] Also in 1970, DOD renamed the MSTS the Military Sealift Command (MSC).[21]

In the Food Security Act of 1985 (P.L. 99-198), Congress increased the requirement for the share of food-aid tonnage shipped on U.S.-flag vessels from 50% to 75%. It also mandated that a certain portion of such cargo be shipped through Great Lakes ports.

In 1996, Congress established the Maritime Security Program (MSP; P.L. 104-239) to replace a similar program that had been in existence since 1936—the Operating Differential Subsidy program (ODS). The MSP provides a flat per-ship operating subsidy intended to offset the higher cost of registering under the U.S. flag. This change from the ODS, whose subsidy rates fluctuated based on the difference between American and foreign crewing costs aboard a particular vessel, was intended to encourage U.S.-flag operators to constrain their operating costs.[22] A study sponsored by MARAD at the time showed that U.S. crew salaries were about three times greater than those aboard vessels sailing under European flags and several times greater than those of Asian-flag ships.[23] Another important difference between the MSP and ODS programs is that MSP carriers are obligated to provide overland transport (to and from ports) to the military in addition to port-to-port ocean transport. Thus, through an operating subsidy, the military gains access to a worldwide commercial distribution network without having to fund the capital costs of that network. In 1997, Congress allowed MSP carriers to carry preference cargoes in foreign-built vessels (P.L. 105-85, §3603(b)). U.S.-flag international operators have stated that without both cargo preference and the MSP there would be no incentive to flag their ships under U.S. registry.

In the FY2009 Defense Act (P.L. 110-417, §3511), Congress granted MARAD the authority to require "make up" cargoes if federal agencies fell short of the percentage of cargo required to be shipped on U.S.-flag vessels and to impose civil penalties.

In 2012, Congress reversed its action of 1985, lowering the required share of food aid that must be carried in U.S.-flag vessels from 75% back to 50% (Moving Ahead for Progress in the 21st Century Act, P.L. 112-141).[24]

Competition between the MSC and the commercial fleet for carriage of military-related cargo has continued. At a recent hearing, a representative of the U.S.-flag shipping industry stated the following:

> DOD must continue to abide by its long-standing "commercial first" policy to provide military cargo to privately owned United States flag vessels when available in lieu of government-owned or controlled vessels. This policy has resulted in military cargo support for the United

States flag fleet, and we strongly urge Congress to ensure that DOD continues its unwavering adherence to this essential policy.

At this same hearing, this witness stated that "United States flag vessels participating in MSP carried more than 90% of the war material to the forward-operating bases during the recent Afghanistan and Iraq conflicts."[25]

Signs of tension between the MSC and private owners of U.S.-flag vessels have appeared periodically. Commercial operators have sought to perform "unrep" missions to resupply Navy ships at sea, but the MSC continues to use its own ships and mariners for these missions. In one instance in the early 1980s, U.S.-flag tanker operators sued the MSC, claiming that it improperly tallied the costs for using its own tankers in order to justify rejecting the bids of private operators, which were much higher.[26] In the late 1980s, the MSC fleet expanded from about 120 vessels to nearly 200, despite the opposition of commercial operators.[27]

In the early 1990s, when two U.S.-flag container carriers, Sea-Land and American President Lines, were threatening to reflag their ships under foreign registry, they called for requiring more military-related shipping activity to be turned over to commercial operators.[28] At this time, there was reportedly an attempt by the Navy to amend the Wilson-Weeks agreement so as to effectively annul it.[29] After the MSC attempted to use one of its own vessels for a large overseas shipment of tanks, legislation was introduced that would have written the Wilson-Weeks agreement into statute.[30] When the MSC began acquiring its own fleet of roll-on/roll-off ships and contested with MARAD over control and administration of the reserve fleet, tensions with the commercial industry increased further.[31] Since the mid-1990s, the MSC fleet has stabilized at around 120 ships, and the focus of U.S.-flag carriers has shifted from containing the size of the MSC fleet to fully funding the MSP program in annual appropriations and to more vigorous enforcement of civilian cargo preferences.

U.S.-flag operators have also been wary of MSC attempts to allow foreign-flag carriers to bid on MSC contracts in an effort to increase competition and obtain lower rates, even though the foreign carriers would have used U.S.-owned ships and U.S. crews.[32]

In recent years, military cargo has accounted for the vast majority of government-sponsored cargo. According to the latest available data compiled by MARAD, in FY2011 military cargo accounted for about 86% of cargo preference tonnage, while food aid accounted for 11% and civilian agency cargoes accounted for 3%.[33] The percentage breakdown of revenue was roughly the same.

Application of Cargo Preference to Imports

Historically, debate over cargo preference requirements has centered primarily on U.S. exports. While the requirements have long been imposed on imports directly impelled by the federal government, such as military equipment and the household goods of service members returning to the United States, they were not enforced on goods imported with federal financial assistance by local or state agencies or private parties.

The FY2009 Defense Act (P.L. 110-417, §3511) specifies that cargo preference requirements apply to cargo that is imported by an organization or person if the federal government "provides financing in any way with federal financial funds for the account of any persons unless otherwise exempted." At least 50% of such cargo must be shipped in U.S.-flag vessels. The law directs the Department of Transportation to issue regulations and guidance to govern the administration of cargo preference by other federal agencies.[34]

While the language was intended to alleviate disputes about the application of cargo preference to particular cargoes, such disputes persist. In 2010, a dispute arose over the application of imported wind turbines financed with Department of Energy Loan Guarantees.[35] MARAD's attempt to apply cargo preference requirements in the 2009 law to vessel components imported for ships constructed with federal loan guarantees has generated objections from commenters who contend that Section 3511 of P.L. 110-417 does not provide MARAD with that authority.[36]

MARAD has not begun a rulemaking process to clarify how the cargo preference requirements of the FY2009 Defense Act will be implemented. The agency submitted a draft notice of proposed rulemaking for Office of Management and Budget approval in December 2011, but the draft notice is still apparently under interagency review and has not been published.[37] The Federal Highway Administration has interpreted the law to apply cargo preference requirements to federally supported highway projects carried out by state departments of transportation and other agencies, but it has not yet issued notification and guidance.[38]

Current State of the U.S.-Flag International Fleet

In 1955, U.S.-flag ships carried about 25% of U.S. foreign trade. Today, their market share is around 1%. The U.S.-flag international fleet has shrunk during this time from 850 ships to 80 ships.[39] Sixty of these ships receive annual Maritime Security Program operating subsidies of $3.1 million each. In return for the subsidies, these 60 ships are to be made available to DOD in times of war or national emergency. The MSP vessels are designated as "militarily useful" by MARAD in consultation with DOD, and are funded from MARAD's budget.[40]

The size of the privately owned fleet fluctuates. As of August 2015, it was about the same size it was in 2000, but in the intervening period it reached a peak of 107 ships in 2011.[41] During the first seven months of 2015, 10 ships left and eight ships joined the fleet.[42] A vessel cannot be transferred to a foreign flag without MARAD's approval unless it no longer receives MSP subsidies or is being replaced with an equally capable vessel.[43] Ships joining the U.S.-flag international fleet would seek a "registry endorsement" from the U.S. Coast Guard, submitting documentation demonstrating U.S. ownership, among other things.[44] Over 30 of the U.S.-flag ships carrying preference cargoes (about 40% of the fleet) were built before 2000. If preference cargoes were not available, they might be scrapped, as likely being too old to be attractive to a foreign-flag carrier.

About 60% of the 80 ships in the fleet are controlled by U.S. entities owned by four large foreign shipping lines (they are permitted as "documentation citizens," as explained below). The ships owned by these entities also make up the majority of the vessels receiving MSP subsidies. The largest operator of U.S.-flag international vessels, Maersk Line, which also owns Farrell Lines, owns 27 U.S.-flag vessels. Most of the U.S. owners not affiliated with a foreign parent company have small fleets under the U.S. flag. Three of them have between five and seven ships each, and about a dozen companies have one or two U.S.-flag ships each. By contrast, the leading foreign-flag containership lines operate hundreds of containerships each, and the largest foreign-flag tanker operators own more than 100 ships each.

Information about the revenues and profits of U.S.-flag international maritime operations is not publicly available. However, it appears that the profitability of U.S.-flag international services is highly dependent on revenues from preference cargos, as many of the operators also use foreign-flag vessels to compete for commercial business.

According to a MARAD study, "U.S.-flag carriers face a significantly higher cost regime than do foreign-flag carriers."[45] This study found that a U.S.-flag containership in international trade, for example, has a daily operating cost that is more than twice that of a foreign-flag containership (see *Table 1*). According to the study, the largest cost difference comes from higher wage costs for U.S.-flag containerships.

Table 1. Daily Operating Costs, U.S. vs Foreign-Flag Containership

(2010)

Cost Categories	U.S.-Flag	Foreign-Flag
Wages	$14,872	$2,698
Stores/Lubes	$1,053	$2,200
Maintenance and Repair	$2,866	$3,237
Insurance	$959	$868
Overhead	$1,444	$581
Total Daily Cost	$21,194	$9,583

Source: MARAD, Comparison of U.S. and Foreign-Flag Operating Costs, September 2011, p. 13.

Note: Wages include basic wages, subsistence, overtime, travel, training, pensions, and union fees.

Several recent developments suggest that the volume of preference cargo may change in the coming years. U.S. food-aid policy has been increasing the use of cash payments and local or regional sourcing of food overseas, potentially reducing food-aid shipments from the United States. The drawdown of forces in Iraq and Afghanistan has reduced military shipments to these regions. The authorization of the Export-Import Bank that generated about 2% of U.S.-flag freight revenue from government-sponsored cargo in 2011 expired on July 1, 2015, although bills reauthorizing the Bank have passed both houses.[46] On the other side of the ledger, an increased U.S. military presence in Asia and the Pacific, where voyages between stations are relatively long, could increase demand for U.S.-flag shipping.[47]

Issues for Congress

Ship Design Needs Diverge

One of the long-standing tenets of U.S. maritime policy is that it is essential to sustain a merchant marine capable of serving military needs in the event of war. The trend toward highly specialized and larger ships in the commercial sector appears inconsistent with the military's shipping needs. In planning for war or national emergencies, the military seeks versatility in terms of where its cargo ships can go and what they can carry, so ships equipped to load and unload diverse cargos in shallow harbors lacking shoreside cranes are preferable. In the commercial sector, smaller mixed-cargo vessels of this sort are typically deployed on trade routes to less developed countries rather than on heavily trafficked routes.

Roll-on/roll-off ships are particularly useful for the military, and they make up a disproportionate share of the vessels eligible for cargo preference. In the commercial market, however, this ship type has evolved into specialized vessel types that do not offer the flexibility the military requires. One example is "pure car carriers," ships designed around the weight and dimension of the passenger automobile and unable to accommodate the wider variety of equipment and supplies for which military sealift may be required. The military also seeks fast ships whose engines are fuel-inefficient relative to commercial carrier needs. Commercial vessels built during the past few years have generally been designed to operate at relatively slow speeds to conserve fuel, and this is potentially inconsistent with military needs.

With these changes in commercial ship designs, the military utility of the U.S. merchant marine may now have more to do with the crews than with the ships themselves. In other words, while merchant ship design may be deviating from military needs, the knowledge and skills of their crews are still transferrable to manning the NDRF or other MSC ships.

CivMar vs. Commercial Mariner Crewing Costs

It may cost more to ship military cargo aboard U.S.-flag commercial vessels than aboard MSC vessels because of a cost differential between federal civilian and commercial mariners. While by law the pay for CivMars must be comparable to the pay of crews in the commercial maritime sector,[48] CivMar compensation lags behind that of commercial crews in other respects. A 2001 study requested by the Navy found that commercial mariner leave earnings were significantly greater than those for CivMars.[49] While commercial mariners typically work six months at sea and receive six months of shore leave during the course of a year, federal civilian mariners typically work at sea nine months and receive three months of shore leave. Thus, filling a billet (one shipboard position) requires two to 2.5 mariners in the commercial fleet and 1.25 in the MSC fleet.[50]

While the same unions that represent commercial mariners also represent civil service mariners, CivMars are not allowed to strike and are not obligated to join a union and pay dues. U.S.-flag shipping lines typically have exclusive contracts with specific maritime unions, and U.S. commercial mariners typically receive their ship assignments through a union hiring hall. The MSC does not negotiate wages and benefits with labor unions; civil service mariner wages and benefits are based on the federal government's General Schedule (GS) pay schedule.[51]

While crew costs are a significant factor in determining shipping costs, they are not the only factor. Vessel-related costs (such as depreciation, insurance, and interest payments) and administrative overhead are difficult to compare between the MSC and private vessel owners because the MSC generally does not account for these costs as the private sector does.[52]

The question of whether MSC or private U.S.-flag ships can provide the least-cost transport for military cargo is a significant one. Budgetary considerations aside, if the objective of sealift policy is merely to sustain the existence of U.S.-controlled and -crewed ships, rather than to maintain a U.S.-flag commercial fleet, that objective can be met equally well whether those ships are government-owned and crewed by federal employees or are privately owned and crewed. However, switching to an entirely government-owned fleet would require making fuller use of MSC-owned vessels or acquisition of additional vessels. Such a change in policy also might reduce the number of mariners available to serve in the RRF if activated.

Ratio of Commercial to Government-Sponsored Cargo

One rationale for supporting privately owned U.S.-flag vessels in international trade is that the government gains access to shipping space through the MSP program by paying only a portion of operating costs ($3.1 million per ship per year) rather than having to purchase and maintain the ships at government expense. In other words, revenue derived from private-sector commercial shippers was expected to finance much of the supply of vessels that DOD might need only intermittently.

MARAD stopped tracking the amount of U.S. waterborne foreign trade carried by U.S.-flag ships in 2003, when it fell below 2% of total tonnage.[53] If preference cargo is now supporting almost all of the costs of the U.S.-flag commercial fleet, then commercial shipments are no longer helping to minimize the government's costs.

One rationale for maintaining a reserve of idle government-owned ships (the RRF and NDRF) is to limit the disturbance to U.S. foreign commerce when a surge in military sealift is needed. The reserve fleet can be activated and additional crew obtained from mariners on shore leave or otherwise inactive without removing commercial vessels from their regular service. However, if the commercial vessels are carrying little private-sector commerce, then the concern that their use for military sealift would disturb U.S. foreign commerce is unwarranted, potentially reducing the necessity for the reserve fleets.[54] This argument presupposes that the capacity of the U.S.-flag international fleet is sufficient for projected military sealift needs and that foreign-flag vessels would not be interested in carrying military cargo.

Competition Among U.S.-Flag Carriers

The small size of the U.S.-flag fleet may limit competition in bidding for preference cargoes.

The 1954 act directs that the requirement that 50% of government-impelled cargoes travel by U.S.-flag ship be calculated separately for each of three vessel categories: dry bulk (e.g., ships carrying grain in bulk form), dry cargo liner (e.g., containerships), and tanker (e.g., ships carrying oil or other bulk liquids). It appears that only seven privately owned U.S.-flag vessels are capable of moving bulk food aid. Of these, four are more than 30 years old, older than the normal 20-year to 25-year economic life of oceangoing ships. The three newer ships are all owned by a single operator.[55]

Lack of competition in the U.S.-flag dry bulk sector has been a persistent concern. In 2000, a proposal to allow a temporary waiver from the three-year wait requirement for foreign-built dry bulk vessels to be eligible to carry preference cargoes was proposed but was not acted upon.[56] In 1970, the ODS program was modified to include dry bulk vessels (since 1936, only liner carriers had been eligible) in order to increase the number of U.S.-flag operators. Dry bulk vessels do not receive MSP subsidies because the military does not ship this type of cargo.

In the container sector, relatively little competition exists among U.S.-flag carriers eligible to carry preference cargos. Although there are three operators in this sector, one of them operates almost two-thirds of the fleet. Dry bulk operators provide limited competition to the containership operators in carrying bagged food aid.

How "Fair and Reasonable" Rates Are Determined

How rates are deemed "fair and reasonable" has a bearing on the cost of U.S.-flag shipping. For different types of preference cargo, Congress has specified whether or not a comparison with world market shipping rates is to be part of a rate reasonableness determination.

Congress specified in the Military Transportation Act of 1904 that rates for military cargo cannot be "excessive or unreasonable" and that U.S.-flag operators cannot charge the military more than they charge private-sector customers for shipping like goods.[57] Based on this language, the military routinely compares proposed U.S.-flag charges with those of foreign-flag operators to determine rate reasonableness. DOD regulations note that the purpose of the 1904 act is to provide a subsidy to U.S.-flag operators, and therefore U.S.-flag operators' charges can be higher than foreign-flag charges, but not excessively so.[58]

For foreign-aid bulk cargo, Congress specified in the Cargo Preference Act of 1954 that U.S.-flag vessels were to be used "to the extent such vessels are available at fair and reasonable rates *for United States-flag commercial vessels*" (italics added). The rate reasonableness standard does not incorporate a comparison with foreign-flag rates. Based on this language, MARAD determines reasonable rates based on its estimate of the cost to U.S.-flag operators for delivering the shipment, plus a reasonable profit.[59] It assumes that the vessel will be returning empty, but makes a cost adjustment if the vessel does carry cargo on the return leg. Under this rate evaluation method, there may not be much incentive for carriers to be efficient—for instance, by investing in more efficient, modern vessels or seeking out commercial cargo, especially if the number of carriers bidding for the cargo, as discussed above, is limited.

For liner carriers (namely containership lines), which, unlike dry bulk vessels, receive MSP operating subsidies to offset higher U.S.-flag operating costs, a comparison with foreign-flag rates is part of the rate reasonableness determination. U.S.-flag liner operators are allowed to earn freight revenues at least equal to what foreign-flag operators would earn for carrying preference cargo.[60] Also, if a U.S.-flag liner operator's rates are published and filed with the Federal Maritime Commission (the agency with regulatory jurisdiction over international liner services), they are automatically considered to be fair and reasonable, irrespective of what a foreign-flag carrier might charge for the same service.[61]

Foreign Parent Companies Questioned

While some U.S.-owned container shipping lines at one time were among the largest and most successful ship lines in the world, these companies with international operations have since been sold to foreign lines. In addition to carrying preference cargoes, most of the former U.S.-owned lines, such as Sea-Land, American President Lines, and Farrell Lines, had ships that participated in the MSP, a program that also has U.S. citizen ownership requirements. Therefore, when these U.S. lines were sold to foreign owners, the new owners set up U.S. entities so that these ships could continue participating in the MSP and cargo preference. Under U.S. shipping law, they qualify as "documentation citizens," which are companies located in the United States and operated by U.S. citizens but with a "foreign parent."[62] The chief executive of the foreign parent company must submit an agreement stating that the parent will not influence the operation of the vessel in a manner adversely affecting the interests of the United States.[63] However, concerns about whether these ships are, in effect, foreign-controlled have been persistent.[64]

In 2013, Liberty Maritime, which sought to enroll two more ships into the MSP program, sued MARAD, claiming that some MSP participants were masquerading as U.S.-owned entities.[65] The U.S. District Court for the Eastern District of New York dismissed the suit, in part on the grounds that it was an inappropriate court of jurisdiction.[66]

Commercial U.S.-Flag Operations in "War Zones "

One of the justifications for government support for a private U.S.-flag fleet is that foreign ships and foreign crews cannot be relied upon to sail into war zones. Several incidents of resistance or refusal involving foreign-flag vessels during and since the Vietnam War appear to support this concern. During the Vietnam War, DOD provided incentive pay for U.S. merchant mariners to sail into war zones.[67] However, it may be the case that a U.S.-flag commercial operator carrying military supplies does not sail to the final port of destination. For instance, a U.S.-flag ship might sail to a hub port in the region of a war zone, where the cargo is transferred to a foreign-flag feeder vessel for movement to a port in, or next to, the war zone. While use of foreign-flag feeder vessels is allowed, to encourage full U.S.-flag service, a carrier that provides U.S.-flag service to the final destination port receives priority in the award of cargo preference bids over bidders that do not.[68]

The U.S.-flag carriers (particularly containership operators) that are affiliated with a large foreign-parent operator may be better equipped to arrange ground transport for U.S. military shipments overseas than the smaller U.S.-flag carriers not affiliated with a foreign parent. Large containership carriers with worldwide operations have been providing these sorts of arrangements for commercial customers since the 1980s, organizing overland transport and storage along with ocean carriage. They have established networks of ground transport providers and are otherwise familiar with peculiarities in moving freight in a particular region. MARAD's Administrator has noted that when Pakistan closed its border during the war in Afghanistan, it was the MSP carriers—that is, mainly the foreign parents of entities operating U.S.-flag vessels—that were able to set up an alternative route for U.S. military supplies, using their contacts with ground transport providers in the overseas region to move cargo to the war zone.[69] Because they do little commercial business, U.S.-flag carriers without foreign parents are unlikely to be able to provide a similar level of service.

Cargo Preference for Oil Shipments?

The boom in U.S. shale oil and natural gas production has led to discussion, particularly in the House Committee on Transportation and Infrastructure, Subcommittee on Coast Guard and Maritime Transportation, about whether to require the use of U.S.-flag tankers for the export of oil and liquefied natural gas (LNG). U.S.-flag shipping interests, including labor unions representing U.S. mariners, have long sought a legal requirement that a portion of U.S. oil trade be shipped on U.S.-flag tankers. With the exception of

Alaska oil (see below), cargo preference has never applied to purely private transactions.

In the 1970s, the focus was whether to apply cargo preference requirements to the importation of oil. In 1974, the Energy Transportation Security Act (ETSA; H.R. 8193, 93rd Congress) would have required that 30% of imported oil be carried in U.S.-flag and U.S.-built tankers. The bill was pocket-vetoed by President Ford. In the 94th Congress (1975), Congress created the Strategic Petroleum Reserve (P.L. 94-163). Since the oil for the reserve is purchased by the federal government, half the oil shipped by vessel must be transported by U.S.-flag tankers pursuant to the Cargo Preference Act of 1954.[70] In the 95th Congress (1977), the ETSA was reintroduced (H.R. 1037, S. 61) with modifications. A version requiring that 9.5% of all U.S. oil imports be carried in U.S.-flag tankers passed the House by voice vote, but was then defeated in a recorded vote of 257 to 165. In the House floor debate, supporters of the bill primarily cited national security and the importance of boosting the domestic shipbuilding base.[71] Members opposing the bill cited costs to consumers, potential retaliation from trading partners, and the political influence of the U.S.-flag shipping industry.[72] That neither DOD nor the Department of State had testified in support of a national security rationale for the bill was also noted in the floor debate. The Senate never took up the measure.

In 1983, a bill was introduced (H.R. 1242, 98th Congress) to require both liquid and dry bulk import and export cargo be transported in U.S.-flag and U.S.-built ships, beginning with 5% the first year and increasing 1% per year until 20% was reached. This bill had 45 House cosponsors. Two hearings were held on the bill, but it received no further action.

In 1995, when Congress lifted the export ban on Alaska North Slope oil (P.L. 104-58), it required that the oil be exported on U.S.-crewed and -flagged tankers, but did not require that the tankers be U.S.-built. At that time, U.S. shipyards and U.S. mariners feared loss of ship repair business and sailing jobs in the absence of a U.S.-flag requirement. (U.S.-flag ships pay a 50% tariff on nonemergency repairs made in foreign yards). After the ban was lifted, roughly 5% to 7% of Alaskan oil was exported, mostly to South Korea, Japan, and China, before exports ceased in 2000.[73]

In 2006, when the United States was still expected to be an importer rather than an exporter of LNG, Congress specified that federal regulators give “top priority” to the processing of licenses for offshore LNG import terminals if they would be supplied by U.S.-flag tankers.[74] LNG shippers contended that requiring U.S.-flag vessels on certain routes would hinder their ability to supply LNG under short-term contracts, which was how LNG was increasingly traded as the global market matured.[75]

U.S. Crewing Costs

The 113th Congress directed MARAD to submit a national maritime strategy toward making U.S. flag vessels more competitive in international shipping, identify federal regulations and policies that reduce U.S.-flag operators' competitiveness, and ensure compliance by federal agencies with cargo preference laws (P.L. 113-281, §603). This same law also required the Coast Guard to initiate a National Academies study of Coast Guard regulations that affect the ability of U.S.-flag vessels to compete effectively (§605).

Among the reasons U.S.-flag shipping is not price-competitive with foreign-flag ships is crewing costs (see *Table 1*). For U.S.-flag ship operators, crewing costs account for about 68% of ship operating costs, compared to 35% for foreign-flag ship operators.[76] From 2000 to 2013, U.S. ship crew wages and salaries roughly doubled in real terms, increasing at roughly three times the rate of all transportation workers.[77] Another factor could be the size of crews. A 1990 study by the National Academies requested by the Coast Guard noted that crew size requirements mandated by statute date back to 1915, when vessels were powered by steam boilers and turbines that required round-the-clock attention.[78] This same statute was also discussed in a 1984 National Academies study requested by MARAD.[79] The statute is still in effect.[80] MARAD's study comparing U.S. and foreign-flag ship operating costs surveyed vessel operators and found that they perceive work rules as requiring larger crews on U.S.-flag vessels.[81] However, MARAD compared the size of crews on ships calling at U.S. ports and found U.S.-flag vessels had slightly smaller crews than foreign-flag ships (but its analysis did not account for vessel size and age—factors in determining crew size).[82]

LEGISLATION IN THE 114TH CONGRESS

Congress is considering several bills that could significantly affect the volume of preference cargo.

H.R. 1987, as passed by the House, would increase MARAD's enforcement of food-aid cargo preference requirements.[83] The bill would raise the share of food aid that must be carried in U.S.- flag ships from 50% to 75%, reversing the reduction that was enacted in the surface transportation act of 2012 (MAP-21).[84] S. 525, sponsored by Senator Corker, the chairman of the Foreign Relations Committee, takes the opposite approach. It would further reduce the U.S.-flag shipping requirement for food aid under Title II of the Food for Peace Act (7 U.S.C. 1721 et seq.) from 50% to 0%, and increase the amount of food aid supplied locally from overseas, thereby decreasing the amount of food aid shipped from the United States.[85] The Administration also supports changes in food-aid policy that would have the effect of reducing U.S.-flag shipments, and sought $25 million in its FY2016 MARAD budget request to “otherwise retain” U.S. merchant mariners. Congress has not approved similar requests in recent years.

Congress is also reauthorizing the Export-Import Bank, almost all of whose financed cargoes are carried on U.S.-flag ships.[86] While the Bank’s authorization expired on July 1, 2015, the House and Senate have passed reauthorization bills.[87]

The National Defense Authorization Act for FY2016 (H.R. 1735), which passed the House and the Senate but was vetoed by President Obama on October 22, 2015,[88] expressed concern for a recent decline in military and food-aid cargoes, and would have increased operating subsidies for MSP carriers from $3.1 million per ship to $3.5 million. H.R. 702, as passed by the House, would increase MSP operating subsidies to about $5 million per ship.

End Notes

[1] U.S. merchant vessels have been utilized since the nation’s first naval conflicts, and this has been stated policy at least since the Merchant Marine Act of 1920 (P.L. 66-261) and the Merchant Marine Act of 1936 (P.L. 74-835), which are codified today at 46 U.S.C. §50101:
(a) Objectives.-It is necessary for the national defense and the development of the domestic and foreign commerce of the United States that the United States have a merchant marine-
(1) sufficient to carry the waterborne domestic commerce and a substantial part of the waterborne export and import foreign commerce of the United States and to provide shipping service essential for maintaining the flow of the waterborne domestic and foreign commerce at all times;
(2) capable of serving as a naval and military auxiliary in time of war or national emergency;
(3) owned and operated as vessels of the United States by citizens of the United States;
(4) composed of the best-equipped, safest, and most suitable types of vessels constructed in the United States and manned with a trained and efficient citizen personnel; and
(5) supplemented by efficient facilities for building and repairing vessels.
(b) Policy. It is the policy of the United States to encourage and aid the development and maintenance of a merchant marine satisfying the objectives described in subsection (a).

[2] http://www.reginfo.gov/public/do/eAgendaViewRule?pubId=201504&RIN=2133-AB74.

[3] Cargo preference does not apply to purely private-sector commercial cargo, 99% of which is imported and exported in foreign-flag ships.

[4] Regarding the shipping costs of food aid, see Government Accountability Office (GAO), International Food Assistance[:] Cargo Preference Increases Food Aid Shipping Costs, and Benefits Are Unclear, GAO-15-666, August 2015; Kenneth Button, Wayne Ferris, and Phillip Thomas, "Food Aid Reforms Will Not Significantly Affect Shipping Industry or Surge Fleet," Center for Public Service, George Mason University, June 2015; Stephanie Mercier and Vincent H. Smith, Military Readiness and Food Aid Cargo Preference: Many Costs and Few Benefits, American Enterprise Institute, September 2015; and Elizabeth R. Bageant, C. Barrett, and E. Lentz, "Food Aid and Agricultural Cargo Preference," Applied Economic Perspectives and Policy (2010), vol. 32(4), pp. 624-641.

[5] There are certain exceptions to the U.S. citizen requirement. For details, see 46 U.S.C. §8103.

[6] The Jones Act was included in the Merchant Marine Act of 1920 (P.L. 66-261).

[7] There are certain exceptions to the U.S. citizen requirement. For details, see 46 U.S.C. §8103.

[8] http://www.marad.dot.gov/resources/data-statistics/. The U.S.-flag international fleet may include some seagoing barges, but MARAD data does not indicate the number, if any.

[9] These are the Navy Working Capital Fund (http://www.secnav.navy.mil/fmc/f mb/Documents/ 15pres/NWCF_Book.pdf) and the Transportation Working Capital Fund (http://www. transcom.mil/documents/annual_reports/ annual_report.pdf).

[10] Oral testimony of MARAD Administrator Paul N. Jaenichen, House Committee on Armed Services, Subcommittee on Seapower and Projection Forces, Hearing—Sealift Force Requirements, July 30, 2014.

[11] Salvatore R. Mercogliano, "Sealift: The Evolution of American Military Sea Transportation" (Ph.D. diss., University of Alabama, 2004), p. 243.

[12] Senate Committee on Interstate and Foreign Commerce, Merchant Marine Study and Investigation, S.Rept. 81-2494, August 30, 1950, p. 62.

[13] Salvatore R. Mercogliano, "Sealift: The Evolution of American Military Sea Transportation" (Ph.D. diss., University of Alabama, 2004), p. 445.

[14] Senate Committee on Interstate and Foreign Commerce, Subcommittee on Merchant Marine and Maritime Matters, Hearing—Merchant Marine Study and Investigation (Transportation of Cargoes by the Military), Part 5, March 21 and 29, 1950, p. 1061.

[15] Liner refers to ships sailing between a series of ports on a regular basis. Today, the term is associated with containerships.

[16] René De La Pedraja, A Historical Dictionary of the U.S. Merchant Marine and Shipping Industry (Westport, CT: Greenwood Press, 1994), p. 660.

[17] Testimony of David T. Matsuda, MARAD Administrator, House Committee on Transportation and Infrastructure, Subcommittee on Coast Guard and Maritime Transportation, "State of the U.S. Merchant Fleet in Foreign Commerce," July 20, 2010. The Administrator testified that along with the Wilson-Weeks agreement, the "National Security Directive on Sealift" (National Security Directive 28, October 5, 1989) governed sealift policy with respect to the use of U.S.-flag commercial vessels.

[18] This act amended the Merchant Marine Act of 1936 (P.L. 74-835), which had directed a federal commission to study and devise means by which U.S. importers and exporters could be induced to use U.S.-flag vessels, gave preference to U.S.-flag vessels for carriage of domestic mail, and required federal employees on official business to travel on U.S.- flag vessels.

[19] See for instance, House Committee on Merchant Marine and Fisheries, "Operations of Military Sea Transportation Service in Relation to Maintenance and Development of the Merchant Marine," H.Rept. 83-2672, August 19, 1954.

[20] Murray A. Bloom, "The Cargo Preference Act of 1954 and Related Legislation," Journal of Maritime Law and Commerce, v. 39, no. 3, July 2008, pp. 290-291.

[21] René De La Pedraja, A Historical Dictionary of the U.S. Merchant Marine and Shipping Industry (Westport, CT: Greenwood Press, 1994), p. 400.

[22] House Committee on National Security, Maritime Security Act of 1995, August 3, 1995, H.Rept. 104-229, p. 9.

[23] H.S. Marcus, P.T. Weber, Massachusetts Institute of Technology, "Competitive Manning of U.S. Flag Vessels," 1994. A 1994 GAO study (Maritime Industry[:] Cargo Preference Laws—Estimated Costs and Effects, November 1994, RCED-95-34, http://www.gao.gov/assets/160/154784.pdf) reported similar results (p. 41).

[24] For further details on recent legislation related to food-aid cargo preference, see CRS Report R41072, U.S. International Food Aid Programs: Background and Issues, by Randy Schnepf.

[25] Written testimony of Niels M. Johnsen, on behalf of USA Maritime, House Committee on Transportation and Infrastructure, Subcommittee on Coast Guard and Maritime Transportation, Hearing—Merchant Marine Issues, September 10, 2014.

[26] "Merchant Fleet Is At War With Navy," Washington Post, July 14, 1983. See also GAO, Industry Concerns Regarding the Policies and Procedures of the Military Sealift Command, T-NSIAD-88-40, August 9, 1988.

[27] This development coincides with the issuance of National Security Directive 28 (October 5, 1989) governing sealift policy, buildup for the Persian Gulf War, and restructuring of the military's transportation command; see Salvatore R. Mercogliano, "Sealift: The Evolution of American Military Sea Transportation" (Ph.D. diss., University of Alabama, 2004), pp. 373-432.

[28] "APL and Sea-Land Want U.S. To Bolster Defense Cargo Pact," Journal of Commerce, March 16, 1992.

[29] "Navy Seeks Cancellation of Preference Agreement, New Pact Gives No Priority to U.S.-Flags," Journal of Commerce, May 9, 1990.

[30] H.R. 57, 103rd Congress. The bill had two cosponsors. Other than a hearing (House Committee on Merchant Marine and Fisheries, Subcommittee on Merchant Marine, Cargo Preference, February 24, 1993), the bill received no further action.

[31] "The Merchant Marine: Time to Strike the Colors," Washington Post, October 5, 1995.

[32] "Defense Contract Bids Raise Questions," Journal of Commerce, August 26, 1997; "Navy Seeks Right to Hire Foreign Shippers," Washington Post, August 29, 1986.

[33] Data on cargo preference tonnage by agency is available in MARAD's annual reports to Congress; http://www.marad.dot.gov/resources/maritime-publications/.

[34] The application of the law to nonfederal entities is codified at 46 U.S.C. §55305. 46 C.F.R. §381.7 indicates cargo preference includes cargoes that are generated by a federal grant, guaranty, loan and/or advance of funds program and applies to the borrower, grantee, and any of their contractors or subcontractors.

[35] "For Some Cargo, DOE Prefers Foreign Flag," Journal of Commerce, October 18, 2010.

[36] 80 Federal Register 22611, April 22, 2015. For comments filed, see http://www.regulations.gov, searching under docket no. "MARAD 2015-0049" and "MARAD 2011-0082." Comments filed by "McKeever - Bloom" and "Overseas Shipholding Group" question MARAD's authority. Comments filed by U.S. shipbuilders and domestic ocean carriers contend that the requirement would severely disrupt shipbuilding supply chains.

[37] http://www.reginfo.gov/public/do/eAgendaViewRule?pubId=201504&RIN=2133-AB74.

[38] Communication from Federal Highway Administration to CRS, October 27, 2015.

[39] As of August 2015.

[40] Congress did not act on an FY2002 budget request to transfer funding of the MSP from the Department of Transportation to DOD.

[41] http://www.marad.dot.gov/resources/data-statistics/.

[42] http://www.marad.dot.gov/wp-content/uploads/pdf/DS_CY15-Flag-Changes-20150821.pdf.

[43] 46 U.S.C. §56101.

[44] 46 U.S.C. §12103, §12111.

[45] MARAD, Comparison of U.S. and Foreign-Flag Operating Costs, September 2011, p. 1.

[46] Based on FY2011 shipments, the latest year available from MARAD; H.R. 22 (Senate-passed) and H.R. 597 (House-passed).

[47] Military Sealift Command, 2013-2018 Strategic Plan, September 2012, p. 14-15; http://www.msc.navy.mil/ publications/MSC_StrategicPlan.pdf.

[48] 5 U.S.C. §5348(a).

[49] CNA, "Is CivMar Compensation Comparable with Industry," Research Memorandum D0003631.A2, May 2001; as summarized in CNA, "Analysis of CivMar Attrition and the Role of Shore Leave, May 2006, p. 5; https://www.cna.org/ CNA_files/PDF/ d0013980.a4.pdf.

[50] Michael Morris, U.S. Naval Institute Proceedings, "We Need More Civil-Service Mariners," October 2001, pp. 76- 79. (The author is an MSC employee.)

[51] Michael Morris, U.S. Naval Institute Proceedings, "We Need More Civil-Service Mariners," October 2001, p. 76-79 (The author is an MSC employee.)

[52] MSC used to perform cost comparisons between use of its own fleet and privately owned vessels, as required by OMB Circular A-76. The methodology used was frequently disputed by U.S.-flag carriers. Congress has forbidden DOD from conducting these cost studies since FY2008; see CRS Report R40854, Circular A-76 and the Moratorium on DOD Competitions: Background and Issues for Congress, by Valerie Bailey Grasso.

[53] http://www.marad.dot.gov/wp-content/uploads/pdf/NMSS_011414_Jaenichen_NMS_S ympo sium_Opening_SLIDES.pdf. No other federal agencies that collect international trade or waterborne freight data appear to track international shipments in U.S.-flag vessels; thus, the government appears to be no longer reporting data that might indicate success in achieving one of the objectives of U.S. maritime policy, that U.S.-flag ships carry a substantial portion of U.S. foreign waterborne commerce (see footnote 1).

[54] In an emergency, cargo preference requirements can be waived (46 U.S.C. §55305(c)), potentially avoiding disturbance to the shipment of preference cargoes.

[55] MARAD fleet statistics; http://www.marad.dot.gov/resources/data-statistics/.

[56] Senate Committee on Commerce, Science, and Transportation; Hearing—Reauthorization of the U.S. Maritime Administration, May 16, 2000.

[57] 10 U.S.C. §2631.

[58] 48 C.F.R. §247.5 (specifically §247.573-1 (c)(3)). A report has to be prepared supporting the contention that U.S.- flag rates are excessive. The Secretary of the Army or the Navy makes the final determination.

[59] 46 C.F.R. §382.

[60] 46 C.F.R. §381.4.

[61] 48 C.F.R. §47.506(c).

[62] 46 C.F.R. §296.10.

[63] 46 C.F.R. §296.3(b)(14).

[64] "Subsidizing Foreign Carriers," Journal of Commerce, October 16, 1997; "American Carriers Are Left Behind In Cargo Program," New York Times, November 20, 2012.

[65] "Liberty Maritime Files Suit Against MARAD," Marine Log, January 24, 2013.

[66] Liberty Global Logistics v. U.S. Mar. Admin., 2014 U.S. Dist. LEXIS 124713 (E.D.N.Y. 2014).

[67] Salvatore R. Mercogliano, "Sealift: The Evolution of American Military Sea Transportation" (Ph.D. diss., University of Alabama, 2004), p. 293.

[68] In one case, a U.S.-flag operator allegedly falsely certified that it hauled exclusively on U.S.-flag vessels when it had transhipped the cargo to foreign flag vessels; Traffic World, "Denying Wrongdoing, APL Agrees To Pay $600,000 To Settle Dispute," March 25, 1996.

[69] Oral testimony of MARAD Administrator Paul N. Jaenichen, House Committee on Armed Services, Subcommittee on Seapower and Projection Forces, Hearing—Sealift Force Requirements, July 30, 2014.

[70] At the time, GAO estimated that U.S.-flag shipping costs would be 2.3 to 2.8 times those of foreign-flag vessels, and questioned whether there was an adequate supply of U.S.-flag tankers. GAO, Transportation Planning For The Strategic Petroleum Reserve Should Be Improved, LCD-78-211, October 18, 1978.

[71] Congressional Record—House, October 19, 1977, p. 34177 et seq.

[72] "The Maritime Payoff," Wall Street Journal, August 4, 1977; "The Great Ship Robbery," New York Times, August 6, 1977; "How To Buy A Bill," Washington Post, September 1, 1977.

[73] U.S. Energy Information Administration, Crude Oil Exports by Destination (as of August 2015); http://www.eia.gov/ dnav/pet/pet_move_expc_a_EP00_EEX_mbbl_m.htm.

[74] P.L. 109-241, §304.

[75] See filings of Shell and the Center for LNG at http://www.regulations.gov under docket no. MARAD-2007-26841.

[76] MARAD, Comparison of U.S. and Foreign-Flag Operating Costs, September 2011, p. 6.

[77] Bureau of Transportation Statistics, National Transportation Statistics, Table 3-26; http://www.rita.dot.gov/bts/sites/rita.dot.gov.bts/files/publications/national_transportation_statistics/html/table_03_26.html.

[78] National Research Council, Crew Size and Maritime Safety (Washington, DC: National Academy Press, 1990), pp. 39-40, 77.

[79] National Research Council, Effective Manning of the U.S. Merchant Fleet (Washington, DC: National Academy Press, 1984), pp. 5, 20-22, 65, 69.

[80] 46 U.S.C. §8104(d) and (e)(1).

[81] MARAD, Comparison of U.S. and Foreign-Flag Operating Costs, September 2011, pp. 6, 43-48.

[82] MARAD, Comparison of U.S. and Foreign-Flag Operating Costs, September 2011, p. 6.

[83] MARAD's mission is to promote the U.S.-flag merchant marine. Indicative of its mission, it was not transferred from the Department of Commerce to the Department of Transportation until 1981, even though the Department of Transportation had been established in 1966 for the purpose of consolidating modal administrations.

[84] H.R. 5769, 113th Congress, as passed by the House, would have increased food-aid cargo preference back to 75%, but the Senate was opposed to the measure, and it was dropped in the final version of the bill.

[85] For further information on food-aid programs and as they relate to cargo preference, see CRS Report R41072, U.S. International Food Aid Programs: Background and Issues, by Randy Schnepf.

[86] See CRS Report R43581, Export-Import Bank: Overview and Reauthorization Issues, by Shayerah Ilias Akhtar.

[87] On July 30, 2015, the Senate passed H.R. 22 with an amendment containing a six-year surface transportation reauthorization, as well as a provision (agreed to by a vote of 64-29) to reauthorize the Bank through FY2019. On October 27, 2015, the House voted (313-118) in favor of H.R. 597, which, as amended, is substantively the same as the Ex-Im Bank extension agreed to by the Senate.

[88] https://www.whitehouse.gov/sites/default/files/omb/legislative/sap/114/saphr1735r_20150 512.pdf.

In: Cargo Preferences for U.S.-Flag Shipping
Editor: Edmund Sutton
ISBN: 978-1-63484-945-6

Chapter 2

INTERNATIONAL FOOD ASSISTANCE: CARGO PREFERENCE INCREASES FOOD AID SHIPPING COSTS AND BENEFITS ARE UNCLEAR*

United States Government Accountability Office

WHY GAO DID THIS STUDY

Cargo preference laws require that a percentage of U.S. government cargo, including international food aid, be transported on U.S.-flag vessels according to geographic area of destination and vessel type. One intention is to ensure a merchant marine—both vessels and mariners— capable of providing sealift capacity in times of war or national emergency, including a full, prolonged activation of the reserve fleet. The CPFA percentage requirement has varied over the years, and was reduced from 75 to 50 percent in 2012. Among other objectives, this report examines (1) CPFA's impact on food aid shipping cost and U.S. agencies' implementation of CPFA requirements and (2) the extent to which the implementation of CPFA requirements contributes to sufficient sealift capacity. GAO analyzed agency documents and bid data from April 2011 (when the food procurement database was implemented) through fiscal

* This is an edited, reformatted and augmented version of the United States Government Accountability Office publication, GAO-15-666, dated August 2015.

year 2014, and interviewed agency officials as well as maritime industry stakeholders.

What GAO Recommends

Recognizing that cargo preference serves statutory policy goals, Congress should consider clarifying CPFA legislation to define "geographic area" in a manner that ensures agencies can fully utilize the flexibility Congress granted to them when it lowered the CPFA requirement. The Secretary of Transportation should direct the Administrator of MARAD to study the potential availability of all qualified mariners needed to meet a full and prolonged activation of the reserve sealift fleet; DOT agreed with this recommendation.

What GAO Found

Cargo preference for food aid (CPFA) requirements increased the overall cost of shipping food aid by an average of 23 percent, or $107 million, over what the cost would have been had CPFA requirements not been applied from April 2011 through fiscal year 2014. Moreover, differences in the implementation of CPFA requirements by the U.S. Agency for International Development (USAID) and U.S. Department of Agriculture (USDA) contributed to a higher shipping rate for USDA. Following the July 2012 reduction in the minimum percentage of food aid to be carried on U.S.-flag vessels, USAID was able to substantially increase the proportion of food aid awarded to foreign-flag vessels, which on average have lower rates, helping to reduce its average shipping rate. In contrast, USDA was able to increase the proportion of food aid awarded to foreign-flag vessels by only a relatively small amount because it is compelled by a court order to meet the minimum percentage of food aid carried on U.S.-flag vessels by individual country, a more narrow interpretation of the geographic area requirement than what USAID applies. Despite GAO's past recommendations, U.S. agencies have not fully updated guidance or agreed on a consistent method for agencies to implement CPFA, which would allow USDA to administer CPFA using a method other than country-by-country.

U.S. Agency for International Development's (USAID) and U.S. Department of Agriculture's (USDA) Cost of Cargo Preference for Food Aid (CPFA) Requirements, April 2011 through Fiscal Year 2014 (Dollars in millions)

	Shipping cost of awarded bids	Estimated shipping cost without CPFA requirements applied	Cost of CPFA requirements	Percentage difference
USAID	$281.5	$236.6	$44.9	16%
USDA	$174.8	$112.6	$62.2	36%
Total	**$456.3**	**$349.2**	**$107.1**	**23%**

Source: GAO analysis of USDA data. | GAO-15-666

Note: USAID's costs do not include shipping of bulk food aid.

CPFA's contribution to sealift capacity is uncertain, and available mariner supply has not been fully assessed. While CPFA has ensured that a portion of U.S.-flag vessels carry some food aid cargo, the number of vessels carrying food aid and U.S. mariners required to crew them has declined. The available pool of sealift capacity has always met all of the Department of Defense's (DOD) requirements, without the full activation of the reserve sealift fleet. DOD's most serious scenario would require a full and prolonged—a period longer than 6 months—activation of the reserve sealift fleet as well as the use of commercial vessels. The Maritime Administration (MARAD) estimated that 3,886 mariners would be needed to crew the reserve surge fleet and 9,148 mariners to crew commercial vessels. MARAD estimated that at least 1,378 additional mariners would be needed to satisfy a full and prolonged activation, including the crewing of commercial vessels. However, the actual number of U.S. mariners qualified and available to fulfill DOD's most serious scenario is unknown and MARAD has not fully assessed the potential availability of all qualified mariners to satisfy a full and prolonged activation.

ABBREVIATIONS

CPFA	cargo preference for food aid
DOT	Department of Transportation
FAS	Foreign Agricultural Service
KCCO	Kansas City Commodity Office
MARAD	Maritime Administration

MOS	Mariner Outreach System
MOU	memorandum of understanding
MSP	Maritime Security Program
NGO	nongovernmental organizations
OFD	Ocean Freight Differential
OLS	Ordinary Least Squares
STCW	Standards of Training, Certification, and Watchkeeping
TPEF	Twenty Percent Excess Freight
VISA	Voluntary Intermodal Sealift Agreement
USAID	U.S. Agency for International Development
USCG	U.S. Coast Guard
USDA	U.S. Department of Agriculture
WBSCM	Web Based Supply Chain Management

***

August 26, 2015

The Honorable Bob Corker
Chairman
Committee on Foreign Relations
United States Senate

The Honorable Edward Royce
Chairman
Committee on Foreign Affairs
House of Representatives

The Honorable Chris Coons
United States Senate

The United States shipped more than 1 million metric tons of food aid in fiscal year 2013, intended to benefit 46.2 million people in 56 countries, at a cost of around $1.7 billion, which included commodity and freight cost. Under U.S. law, a minimum share of U.S. food aid must be shipped on U.S.-flag vessels. For the purposes of the report, we refer to that requirement as cargo preference for food aid (CPFA).[1] The percentage requirement of CPFA has fluctuated since 1954, from the original 50 percent to 75 percent in 1985, and back to 50 percent in 2012. The U.S. Agency for International Development

(USAID) and the U.S. Department of Agriculture (USDA) administer food aid programs; the cost of transporting food aid comes from the funding for these programs. The Department of Transportation's (DOT) Maritime Administration (MARAD) is responsible for monitoring USAID's and USDA's adherence to CPFA. Statutory objectives for cargo preference, which in addition to food aid are also applied to other government cargo such as Department of Defense (DOD) cargo, include the development and maintenance of a merchant marine—both vessels and mariners—capable of providing sealift in time of war or national emergency.[2] According to MARAD officials, the objectives for CPFA are the same as the statutory objectives for cargo preference in general.

In response to your request, in this report, we examine (1) CPFA's impact on food aid shipping cost and U.S. agencies' implementation of CPFA requirements, (2) the extent to which the implementation of CPFA requirements contributes to sufficient sealift capacity, and (3) stakeholder views on options to improve the sustainability of the oceangoing U.S.-flag fleet.[3]

To address our objectives, we analyzed cargo preference legislation as well as USAID's, USDA's, and MARAD's guidance and data on CPFA. We also interviewed USAID, USDA, and MARAD officials about each agency's roles and responsibilities regarding CPFA, the processes each agency uses to implement CPFA and to ensure and monitor compliance with the requirements, the cost implications of the requirements on food aid programs, and the impact of the requirements on cargo preference objectives.[4] To determine the CPFA requirements' impact on food aid shipping cost, we analyzed food aid procurement data for both USAID and USDA from April 2011 through fiscal year 2014, including some bulk food commodities and all packaged food commodities and shipment data for fiscal years 2011 through 2014.[5] During this time period, CPFA requirement levels changed from 75 to 50 percent. We examined the number of total U.S.-flag and foreign-flag bids per solicitation. We used regression analysis to identify the impact of the changes in the CPFA requirements. To examine the extent to which the implementation of CPFA requirements contributes to sufficient sealift capacity, we interviewed DOD officials about the sealift capability and military usefulness of the vessels in the U.S.-flag fleet. We also analyzed MARAD's data on U.S.-flag vessels, including those carrying food aid cargo and the number of mariner positions aboard such vessels. Furthermore, we obtained data from the U.S. Coast Guard (USCG) on the number of mariners potentially qualified to provide sealift during times of war or national emergencies. We found the data on U.S.-flag vessels, mariner positions supported by CPFA, and mariners that crewed the Ready Reserve Force from 2002 to 2015 sufficiently reliable for the purposes of this report. We also interviewed MARAD officials to understand the crewing process for the reserve sealift fleet. MARAD officials described the data they used and factors they considered to estimate the number of positions needed for a full, prolonged operation of the reserve surge fleet and all commercial vessels and the number of available mariners. However, we were not able to assess the accuracy of these estimates because MARAD was unable to provide us with the details about them. To obtain stakeholder views on options to improve the sustainability of the oceangoing U.S.-flag fleet, we conducted semistructured interviews and requested follow-up documentation from a nongeneralizable sample of 29 stakeholders knowledgeable about CPFA issues, selected based on, among other factors, how often others suggested we meet with them and their location.[6] We categorized these stakeholders into (1) maritime industry stakeholders, which are those stakeholders that we interviewed that self-identified as brokers, carriers, freight forwarders, and mariners, and (2) other maritime stakeholders, which are those stakeholders that we interviewed that self-identified as academia, commodities, freight forwarders, implementing partners or nongovernmental organizations (NGO),[7] ports, and trade associations.[8] The intent of our semistructured interviews was to identify options to improve the sustainability of the oceangoing U.S.-flag fleet, including food aid-carrying U.S.-flag vessels. We did not specifically ask stakeholders to consider the effect that options may have on food aid. Twenty of the 29 stakeholders we interviewed responded to our follow-up request. Eighteen of these stakeholders (7 maritime industry stakeholders and 11 other maritime stakeholders) selected what they believe to be the top three options from among those suggested and provided comments on a variety of the options, while the other 2 stakeholders (both other maritime stakeholders) responded that they would not provide their views because they did not favor any of the options.[9] See appendix I and II for more details on our scope and methodology, as well as our regression methodology and results.

We conducted this performance audit from October 2014 to August 2015 in accordance with generally accepted government auditing standards. Those standards require that we plan and perform the audit to obtain sufficient, appropriate evidence to provide a reasonable basis for our findings and conclusions based on our audit objectives. We believe the evidence obtained provides a reasonable basis for our findings and conclusions based on our audit objectives.

BACKGROUND

Evolution of the Legal Requirements of Cargo Preference for Food Aid

The legal requirements of CPFA, particularly the required level of CPFA shipped on U.S.-flag vessels, have changed over time. Figure 1 shows key legislation related to CPFA.

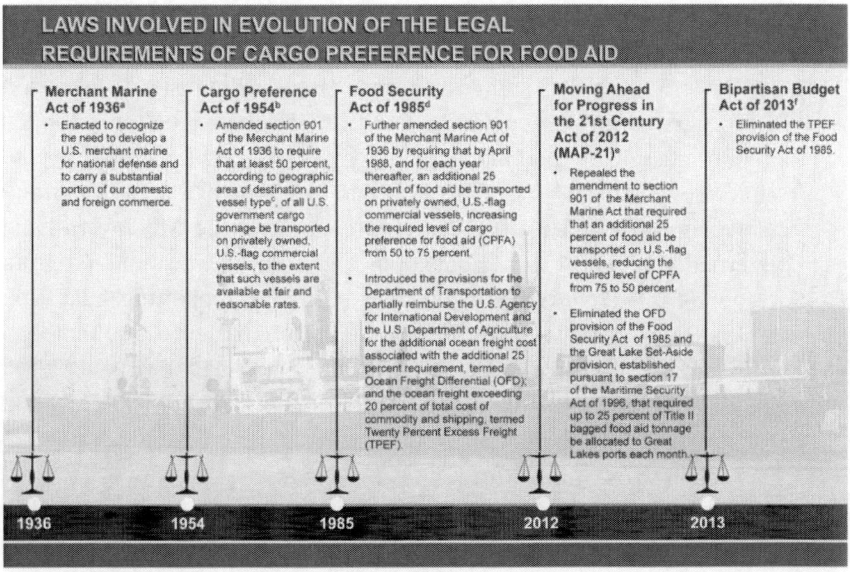

Source : GAO analysis of laws. | GAO-15-666

[a] Act of June 29, 1935, ch. 858.

[b] Act of Aug. 26, 1954, ch. 936 codified at 46 USC 55305.

[c] The three types of vessels are dry bulk carriers, dry cargo liners, and tankers. The distinction between bulk carriers and cargo liners is the service provided by the vessel. Dry bulk carriers provide irregular service to a destination port, while dry cargo liners provide regularly scheduled service. Tankers are vessels used primarily for the carriage of bulk liquid cargoes such as liquid petroleum products, vegetable oils, and molasses.

[d] Pub. L. No. 99-198.

[e] Pub. L. No. 112-141, Div. F, § 100124.

[f] Pub. L. No. 113-67, Div. A, § 602.

Figure 1. Timeline of Key Laws Involved in Evolution of the Legal Requirements of Cargo Preference for Food Aid.

Roles of Various U.S. Agencies Involved in CPFA

USAID, USDA, and MARAD are the primary agencies involved in CPFA.

- USAID administers Title II of the Food for Peace Act, which responds to emergency needs such as disasters and crises, and targets the underlying causes of hunger and malnutrition through development food assistance programs. In fiscal year 2014, USAID provided an estimated 1 million metric tons of food aid valued at more than $1.3 billion.
- USDA's Foreign Agricultural Service (FAS) administers other food aid programs. In particular, the Food for Progress program responds to non-emergency food aid situations by supporting agricultural value chain development, expanding revenue and production capacity, and increasing incomes in food-insecure countries. The McGovern-Dole International Food for Education and Child Nutrition program responds to nonemergency food aid needs by supporting education and nutrition for schoolchildren, particularly girls, expectant mothers, and infants. In fiscal year 2014, USDA provided nearly 192,000 metric tons of food aid, valued at more than $127 million, for Food for Progress; and more than 70,000 metric tons of food aid, valued at more than $164 million, for McGovern-Dole.
- USDA's Farm Service Agency serves as the buying agent for all U.S. food aid programs and extends invitations for bids to prospective food commodities sellers and providers of freight services for commodity delivery to overseas ports. The Farm Service Agency's Kansas City Commodity Office (KCCO) is responsible for procuring food commodities.
- MARAD is responsible for monitoring federal agencies' implementation of cargo preference laws, including CPFA. In addition to monitoring compliance, MARAD establishes guideline rates to determine whether U.S.-flag shipping rates are fair and reasonable. See appendix III for details on MARAD's "fair and reasonable" determinations.

DOD and the USCG also have some involvement in CPFA, through various activities detailed below.

Voluntary Intermodal Sealift Agreement and Maritime Security Program

DOD has programs that involve U.S.-flag vessels that compete to ship food aid under CPFA. For example, the Voluntary Intermodal Sealift Agreement (VISA) is a partnership between the U.S. government and the maritime industry to provide DOD with "assured access" to commercial sealift and intermodal capacity to support the emergency deployment and sustainment of U.S. military forces.[10] During times of war or national emergency, DOD will use commercial sealift capacity, to the extent it is available, to meet ocean transportation requirements. This commercial sealift capacity includes U.S.- and foreign-flag vessels or intermodal capacity to support DOD's needs. In the event voluntary capacity does not meet DOD contingency requirements, DOD will activate VISA as necessary. VISA participants have committed vessels or intermodal capacity to support DOD contingency requirements during the various activation stages of VISA and in return are afforded priority to meet DOD peacetime and contingency sealift requirements.

Vessels participating in the Maritime Security Program (MSP) are required to be enrolled in VISA.[11] MSP is intended to guarantee that certain kinds of militarily useful ships and their crews will be available to DOD in a military contingency. Vessels in MSP will be activated through the VISA program. Currently, MSP provides direct payment of up to $3.1 million per year for up to 60 militarily useful U.S.-flag vessels participating in international trade to support DOD. DOT determines the commercial viability and DOD determines the military usefulness of vessels that seek participation in MSP. Guidance on military usefulness is being updated and is expected to be issued by September 2015.[12] According to DOD officials, the criteria for military usefulness include ship speed, deck strength, and container cargo carriage capacity.[13]

Reserve Sealift Fleet

DOD, through the United States Transportation Command, and DOT, through MARAD, maintain and operate a fleet of vessels owned by the federal government to meet the logistic needs of the military services that cannot be met by existing commercial service. As of July 2015, the reserve sealift fleet is composed of 61 vessels, 46 of which are MARAD- owned and form part of the Ready Reserve Force,[14] and 15 are DOD- owned vessels in the Military Sealift Command's Surge Sealift program. DOD notifies the Military Sealift Command and MARAD when it directs activation of vessels in the reserve sealift fleet for contingency operations, exercises, training and testing, and other defense purposes for when commercial sealift is not available or suitable. Such vessels must be fully operational with a complete crew within their assigned readiness status, which varies from 5 to 10 days.[15] Commercial U.S. ship managers provide systems maintenance, equipment repairs, logistics support, activation, manning, and operations management by contract.

U.S. Mariners

U.S. mariners are necessary to crew U.S.-flag commercial vessels providing sealift capabilities for DOD needs, as well as the reserve sealift fleet. Crewing of such vessels is a voluntary system for mariners with the necessary qualifications. Mariner qualifications for crewing the reserve sealift fleet include having a USCG merchant mariner credential with the necessary national and international endorsements to crew these vessels, which include Standards of Training, Certification and Watchkeeping (STCW) and endorsement for unlimited tonnage for deck officer positions that include master, chief mate and officer in charge of a navigational watch, and unlimited horsepower for engineer positions.[16] In addition, mariners sailing onboard such vessels, among other things, are required to take specific DOD-approved training matching their types of vessels, cargo, mission requirements, and areas of operation, according to MARAD. The specialized training includes topics such as physical security, antiterrorism, ship survivability, Navy communication systems, naval operations, engineering, and logistics.[17] This training is typically provided by Navy trainers, as well as by union and private trainers. Currently, U.S. maritime labor unions have collective bargaining agreements with vessel operators under contract to the government to crew the reserve sealift fleet, as needed. USCG is responsible for the credentialing of mariners and maintains records on all mariners who hold valid merchant mariner credentials, including data on mariners who may serve on U.S.-flag vessels that support DOD during times of war or national emergencies, among which are vessels that compete to ship food aid under CPFA.

Strategic Sealift Officer Program

The Navy's Strategic Sealift Officer Program maintains within the Reserve Component of the U.S. Navy a cadre of strategic sealift officers to support national defense sealift requirements and capabilities. Strategic sealift officers can be recalled to active military duty to fill officer positions aboard the reserve sealift fleet if a shortage of qualified civilian mariners exists. However, many of the Strategic Sealift Officers may already be employed as civilian mariners onboard commercial vessels. The Navy and MARAD have agreed that Strategic Sealift Officers may be used to fill officer positions aboard the reserve sealift fleet after all reasonable means to obtain other qualified civilian mariners have been exhausted.

Food Aid Purchasing and Shipping Process

USAID and USDA rely on implementing partners to deliver food aid to beneficiaries for emergency and nonemergency purposes.[18] Implementing partners submit a food order proposal designed to meet program objectives of USAID's and USDA's food aid programs. USAID and USDA officials review the order to ensure its suitability for the program and country area with regard to the quantity and type of commodity requested. Once approved, the commodity request for food aid is forwarded to KCCO, which collects commodity orders with similar delivery dates for placement on a solicitation.[19] KCCO then issues a solicitation for commodity vendors to offer their products for sale to USDA. Concurrently, administering agencies, working with implementing partners, issue a solicitation with specific freight tender terms and conditions for ocean freight services to deliver these commodities to overseas destinations. For all U.S. in-kind food commodities except USAID's bulk food aid, ocean carriers and commodity vendors submit offers electronically through the Web Based Supply Chain Management system (WBSCM).[20] KCCO evaluates commodity bids and freight offers according to lowest landed cost (the cost of the commodity plus transportation charges), through WBSCM. USAID and USDA review the ocean freight offers to identify programmatic issues, such as ensuring ocean freight offers meet the tenders' terms and conditions, ensuring rates are consistent with fair market prices, as well as assessing the offers' relation with CPFA requirements. USAID and USDA coordinate with KCCO to recommend award of commodity and transportation contracts, and advise the implementing partners to enter into such contracts.[21]

Shipping Rates on U.S.- Flag versus Foreign-Flag Vessels

U.S.-flag vessels charge higher shipping rates than foreign-flag vessels largely because of their higher operating cost. According to a MARAD study, U.S.-flag vessels face significantly higher cost, including crew cost, maintenance and repair cost, insurance cost, and overhead cost.[22] For 2010, MARAD found that the average U.S.-flag vessel operating cost is roughly 2.7 times higher than its foreign-flag counterpart. MARAD also found that crew cost, the largest component of U.S.-flag vessels' operating cost, was about 5.3 times higher than that of foreign-flag vessels. While crew cost accounted for about 70 percent of U.S.-flag vessel operating cost, it accounted for about 35 percent for the foreign- flag vessels.

DOD Determines Sealift Capacity Needs and MARAD Assesses Sufficiency of the Mariner Pool

National Security Directive 28 directs DOD to determine the requirements for sealift, among other things, and DOT to determine whether adequate manpower is available to meet such requirements. According to DOD officials, DOD has determined the number of vessels, including those in the reserve sealift fleet that would be required to meet its needs under different contingency scenarios and communicated that to MARAD. DOD officials told us that the number of vessels—both commercial and those in the reserve sealift fleet—required to meet sealift capability for DOD needs varies by contingency. However, DOD's most serious scenario requires a full and prolonged—a period longer than 6 months—activation of the reserve sealift fleet as well as the use of commercial vessels. MARAD analyzes USCG data, vessel information data, and talks to U.S. maritime labor unions to estimate the number of U.S. mariners actively sailing to determine whether sufficient U.S. mariners exist to crew the entire reserve sealift fleet as well as maintain commercial operations.

Cargo Preference Requirements Increase Food Aid Shipping Costs, Especially for USDA

CPFA requirements increased the cost of shipping food aid for USAID and USDA by about 23 percent, or $107 million, over what it would have been had CPFA requirements not been applied during the time period April 2011 through fiscal year 2014.[23] USDA pays higher shipping rates than USAID partly because of the different application of the CPFA requirements between the two agencies. Pursuant to a court order following a law suit filed against USDA, USDA must measure compliance with cargo preference laws for Food for Progress and Section 416(b) programs on a country-by-country basis to the extent practicable unless MARAD revises cargo preference regulations or policy to allow a different method for defining geographic area, or if USDA determines that a change in method is necessary following good faith negotiations on the matter with MARAD. The country-by-country basis is a more narrow interpretation of the geographic area requirement associated with CPFA than what USAID applies. Following the July 2012 reduction in the minimum percentage of food aid to be carried on U.S.-flag vessels from 75 percent to 50 percent, USAID was able to substantially increase the proportion of food aid awarded to foreign-flag vessels, helping to reduce its average shipping rate. In contrast, USDA was only able to increase the proportion of food aid awarded to foreign-flag vessels by a relatively small amount such that it utilized foreign-flag vessels far below the 50 percent allowed by the 2012 law, and its average shipping rate did not decrease. USAID and USDA continue to differ in how they implement CPFA, and they, together with MARAD, have not fully updated guidance for or agreed on a consistent method for agencies to implement CPFA based on geographic area.

Cargo Preference Requirements Increase Total Shipping Costs, but USAID and USDA No Longer Receive Reimbursements to Compensate for the Higher Cost

The cargo preference requirements for food aid increased the total cost of shipping food aid (see table 1). We found that CPFA requirements increased the cost of shipping food aid by 23 percent, increasing the total cost of shipping food aid by $107 million. This increase covers all of USDA's food aid purchases and USAID's purchases of packaged food aid from April 2011 through fiscal year 2014.[24] The extra cost to meet the CPFA requirements was $45 million for USAID's packaged food aid, 16 percent higher than what USAID would have paid if the CPFA requirements were not applied for April 2011 through fiscal year 2014.[25] For USDA's food aid, the extra cost was $62 million, or 36 percent higher.

Table 1. Shipping Costs with Cargo Preference for Food Aid (CPFA) Requirements and Estimated Costs if CPFA Requirements Were Not Applied for Food Aid Shipped, from April 2011 through Fiscal Year 2014 (Dollars in millions)

	Shipping cost of awarded bids	Estimated shipping cost if CPFA requirements were not applied	Cost of CPFA requirements	Percentage difference
U.S. Agency for International Development (USAID)	$281.5	$236.6	$44.9	16%
U.S. Department of Agriculture (USDA)	$174.8	$112.6	$62.2	36%
Total	**$456.3**	**$349.2**	**$107.1**	**23%**

Source: GAO analysis of U.S. Department of Agriculture (USDA) data. | GAO-15-666

Note: USAID's costs do not include shipping of bulk food aid. For each solicitation of USAID's packaged and USDA's packaged and bulk food aid, KCCO has data on the bids that were awarded the shipping contract as well as the bids that would have been awarded the contract if the CPFA requirements were not applied. The difference between the two is a measure of the cost of meeting the CPFA requirements.

The Food Security Act of 1985 raised the CPFA requirement from 50 percent to 75 percent and required DOT to reimburse USAID and USDA for the ocean freight cost associated with the additional 25 percent requirement, and for the portion of the freight cost that exceeded 20 percent of total commodity and freight cost (see table 2).[26] These two reimbursements—Ocean Freight Differential (OFD) and Twenty Percent Excess Freight (TPEF)—ranged from around $50 million to over $100 million a year from fiscal years 2010 to 2012. Agencies used the reimbursement to fund additional food aid programs. After the CPFA requirement was lowered in July 2012, USAID and USDA still incurred the extra cost to meet the requirements but they no longer received any reimbursement. According to a USDA official, it funds about three fewer grant agreements per year after the reimbursements stopped because of the loss of reimbursements. From fiscal years 2009 through 2012, USDA signed an average of 35 new grant agreements a year amounting to around $388 million a year. For fiscal years 2013 and 2014, USDA signed an average of about 20 new grant agreements a year amounting to around $313 million a year.

Table 2. Ocean Freight Differential (OFD) and Twenty Percent Excess Freight (TPEF) Reimbursements for the U.S. Agency for International Development (USAID) and U.S. Department of Agriculture (USDA), Fiscal Years 2010 to 2012 (Dollars in millions)

	USAID			USDA			Total
Fiscal year	TPEF	OFD	USAID Total	TPEF	OFD	USDA Total	
2010	$86	$6	$92	$20	$0.06	$20	**$112**
2011	$24	$16	$39	$4	$5	$9	**$49**
2012	$33	$18	$51	$8	$5	$13	**$64**

Source: GAO analysis of U.S. Agency for International Development (USAID) and U.S, Department of Agriculture (USDA) data. | GAO-15-666

Note: Figures in the table may not add up to total because of rounding.

Different Implementation of Geographic Area Leads to Higher Shipping Rates Paid by USDA

Geographic Area Is Undefined in Law, Leading to Differing Agency Implementation

USAID and USDA use different interpretations of how to implement CPFA requirements, which contributed to the substantial differences in shipping rates between them. The Cargo Preference Act of 1954 specified that at least 50 percent of the gross tonnage of U.S. food aid commodities be shipped on U.S.-flag vessels "in a manner that will ensure a fair and reasonable participation of commercial vessels of the United States in those cargoes by geographic areas."[27] However, neither this act and subsequent laws modifying the CPFA minimum percentage requirement nor the cargo preference regulations promulgated by MARAD define geographic area. In 1998, the United States District Court for the District of Columbia ordered USDA to measure compliance with cargo preference laws for Food for Progress and Section 416(b) programs on a country-by-country basis to the extent practicable unless MARAD revises cargo preference regulations or policy to allow a different method for defining geographic area, or if USDA determines that a change in method is necessary following good faith negotiations on the matter with MARAD.[28] Thus, USDA is required to meet the minimum percentage of food aid carried on U.S.-flag vessels by individual country and for each of its food assistance programs, which are Food for

Progress and McGovern-Dole, regardless of the price of U.S. shipping, according to USDA officials. USAID, however, is not bound by the order as it was not a party to the litigation. Instead, USAID interprets the CPFA requirement in a manner that gives it substantially more flexibility. It defines geographic area on a global basis for its packaged food aid. For bulk food aid, USAID uses a modified country basis where it can broaden the interpretation of geographic area to the regional level when it determines that there is limited availability of U.S.-flag vessels for a particular route. For example, USAID defines the region of West Africa, and not individual countries in West Africa, as one geographic area for bulk food aid, giving it greater flexibility and allowing it to better manage its limited resources.

USDA Shipped a Lower Proportion of Food Aid on Foreign-Flag Vessels than USAID

USDA shipped a lower percentage of food aid on foreign-flag vessels than USAID, and its percentage on U.S.-flag vessels was higher than the minimum requirements both before and after the 2012 changes in the CPFA requirements. In addition, it did not reduce the percentage on U.S.- flag vessels as much as USAID did after the change in CPFA requirements in July 2012 (see figure 2). We analyzed data on USAID's and USDA's food aid shipments from fiscal years 2009 through 2014 and found that USAID shipped an average of 82 percent of food aid on U.S.- flag vessels before the change and 54 percent after the change. In contrast, USDA shipped an average of 89 percent of food aid on U.S.-flag vessels before the change and 76 percent after the change.

According to USDA officials, USDA ships a high percentage of its food aid on U.S.-flag vessels because it has to meet the minimum percentage shipped on U.S.-flag vessels by country, and its shipments are generally too small to be split among multiple vessels. Our analysis found that U.S.- flag vessels carried at least 50 percent of the commodities to 20 out of the 21 countries USDA sent food aid to in 2014 (see figure 3). In contrast, U.S.- flag vessels carried over 50 percent of the commodities to only 19 out of 31 countries USAID sent food aid to in 2014. When considering the vessel type separately, we found that U.S.-flag vessels carried 100 percent of the food aid shipped on either bulk or liner for 9 out of the 21 countries that USDA sent food aid to in 2014. We examined the countries with 100 percent USDA food aid shipments on U.S.-flag vessels and found all of them received only one shipment of food aid in that year for the particular vessel type. USDA had no choice but to use U.S.-flag vessels when it had only one shipment to a country in a given year because of the way it is legally required to interpret geographic area. For example in 2014, USDA shipped 100 percent of its food aid, consisting of only one shipment each year, to the Dominican Republic using U.S.-flag vessels. When USDA had multiple shipments to a country, such as to Ethiopia in 2014, it was able to send some food on foreign-flag vessels. For USAID, U.S.-flag vessels, either bulk or liner, carried 100 percent of the food aid for 9 out of the 31 countries USAID sent food aid to in 2014.

Average Shipping Rate Decreased for USAID but Not for USDA after the Changes in the CPFA Requirements

We found that after the changes in the CPFA requirements, the average shipping rate for USAID decreased by around 9 percent, or $21 per metric ton, after controlling for other factors. The shipping rate decreased slightly for USDA, though the decrease is not statistically significant. Since a variety of factors in addition to the changes in the CPFA requirements may affect shipping rates, we developed multivariate regression models that control for other factors that may also affect shipping rates to assess the likely effect of the changes.[29] For detailed discussion of the regression methodology and results, see appendix II.

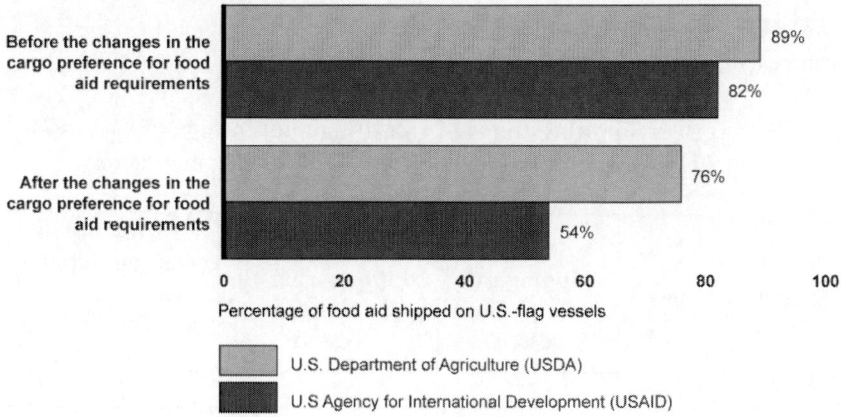

Source: GAO analysis of USDA data. | GAO-15-666

Figure 2. Percentages of U.S. Agency for International Development (USAID) and U.S. Department of Agriculture (USDA) Food Aid Shipped on U.S.-Flag Vessels, Fiscal Years 2009-2014.

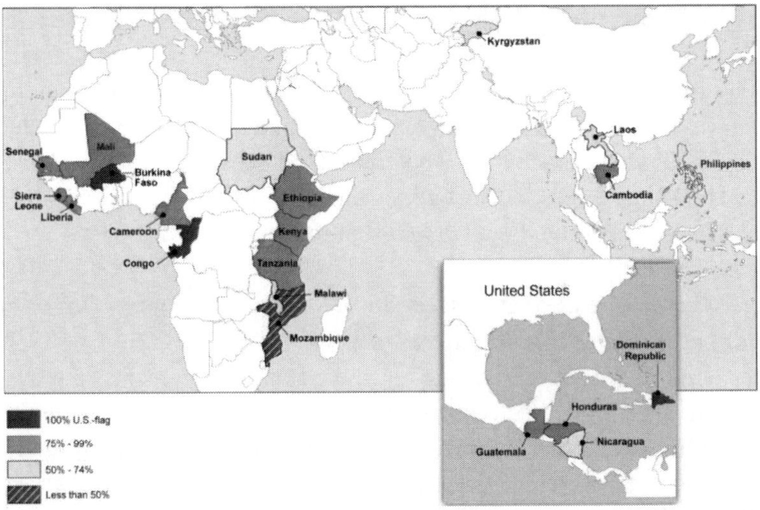

Source: GAO analysis of U.S. Department of Agriculture data; Map Resources (map). | GAO-15-666

Note: In fiscal year 2014, two relatively large bulk shipments to Mozambique did not receive any bids from U.S.-flag vessels and were awarded to foreign-flag vessels. This resulted in less than 50 percent of food aid to Mozambique being shipped on U.S.-flag vessels that year.

Figure 3. Percentage of Food Aid Shipped on U.S.-Flag Vessels for 2014 U.S. Department of Agriculture (USDA) Programs.

Table 3. Average Shipping Rates of U.S.-Flag and Foreign-Flag Vessels, April 2011 through Fiscal Year 2014 (Dollars per metric ton)

Type of food aid	Average shipping rate on U.S.-flag vessels	Average shipping rate on foreign-flag vessels	Difference in average shipping rates on U.S.- and foreign-flag vessels
Packaged food aid	$245	$184	$61
Bulk food aid	$153	$98	$55

Source: GAO analysis of U.S. Department of Agriculture (USDA) data. | GAO-15-666

A higher proportion of food aid awarded to foreign-flag vessels and the decrease in shipping rates on foreign-flag vessels likely contributed to the lower shipping rates for USAID after the CPFA requirement change in 2012. Foreign-flag vessels on average charge lower shipping rates than U.S.-flag vessels (see table 3). From April 2011 through fiscal year 2014, we found that U.S.-flag vessels charged $61 ton more than foreign flag vessels for packaged food aid and $55 per metric ton more for bulk food aid. After the CPFA requirement change, foreign-flag vessels participated more in the food aid solicitation. Our estimates using statistical modeling to control for various factors show that the number of bids received for each solicitation increased by three after the 2012 change in the CPFA requirements and that all of the increase was from the increase in bids from foreign-flag vessels. According to USAID officials, after the CPFA requirement change, they have received more foreign-flag bids for some routes previously dominated by U.S.-flag vessels. Results from our regression model also indicates that the shipping rate on foreign-flag vessels decreased by 9 percent for USAID and 7 percent for USDA since the CPFA requirement change in 2012. USAID was able to award more food aid shipments to lower-priced foreign-flag vessels, which led to a statistically significant decrease in its overall shipping rates. On the other hand, USDA was able to increase the proportion awarded to foreign-flag vessels by a relatively small amount and we did not find a statistically significant decrease in its overall shipping rates since the CPFA requirement change in 2012.

Agencies Have Not Agreed on Updated Guidance for CPFA

MARAD, USAID, and USDA do not have updated guidance and have not agreed on a consistent method for the agencies to implement CPFA. They signed a memorandum of understanding (MOU) in 1987 for administering CPFA that, among other things, did not provide an agreed- upon definition for geographic area. They signed another MOU in 2009 that relates to the interpretation of vessel service categories but still left the definition of geographic area unaddressed. Officials representing the agencies told us that they could not successfully agree on some cargo preference issues. The three agencies currently use separate agency guidance to interpret application of CPFA requirements, but do not follow a common set of updated interagency guidance. According to MARAD, USAID, and USDA officials, they know about the different process each agency uses to implement CPFA, but these practices are not documented in any interagency guidance. MARAD officials said that they regularly monitor USAID's and USDA's compliance with CPFA, based on vessels' voyage report data and the data that USAID and USDA report on their websites. However, MARAD officials also explained that it is difficult for them to enforce CPFA requirements, noting that they understand that USAID uses a different interpretation of geographic area for CPFA compliance of USAID's packaged food aid. Although there is the potential for a $25,000 fine per day for each willful violation of the cargo preference requirement, MARAD officials said that even if they found instances of non-compliance, they cannot penalize USAID and USDA, because they are government agencies. Rather, they would have to penalize the implementing partner that ships the commodities for noncompliance, which they have chosen not to do. In past proposals to MARAD for cargo preference rule making, USDA noted that one of the topical areas of most concern to USDA for its food aid shipments is the definition of the term "geographic areas." USDA had also noted that USDA and USAID needed clarity on the application of CPFA to allow for efficient and effective delivery of food aid.

Our prior work found that agencies that articulate their agreements in formal documents can strengthen their commitments to working collaboratively. Specifically related to CPFA, GAO recommended in 2007 and again in 2009 that USAID and USDA work with DOT and relevant parties to expedite updating the MOU between U.S. food assistance agencies and DOT to minimize the cost impact of cargo preference regulations on food aid transportation expenditures and to resolve uncertainties associated with the application of CPFA requirements.[30] The agencies did not fully implement our recommendation; their signed MOU in 2009 did not resolve some uncertainties among agencies, including the definition of geographic area. Pursuant to the terms of the court order requiring USDA to comply with CPFA on a country-by-country basis, an MOU embodying an agreement between USDA and MARAD on a consistent definition of "geographic area" would allow USDA to administer CPFA using a method other than country-by-country.

CPFA's Contribution to Sealift Capacity Is Uncertain, and MARAD Has Not Fully Considered Available Mariner Supply

Despite cargo preference, the number of vessels carrying food aid and U.S. mariners required to crew them has declined. However, DOD has met all of its past sealift needs with the existing capacity and has never fully activated the reserve sealift fleet. The number of U.S. mariners qualified and available to serve DOD's needs under a full and prolonged activation is uncertain. Furthermore, MARAD has not fully assessed the sufficiency of mariners available under a full and prolonged activation.

Despite Cargo Preference, the Number of Vessels Carrying Food Aid and U.S. Mariners Required to Crew them Has Declined

Sealift capability provided by U.S.-flag vessels, including those carrying food aid, has declined. From 2005 to 2014, the number of vessels in the overall oceangoing U.S.-flag fleet declined about 23 percent, from 231 to 179 vessels.[31] In April 2015, MARAD reported that the decrease in available government cargo is the most significant factor contributing to the loss of U.S.-flag vessels.[32] The majority of the decline has been in DOD cargo, the largest source of preference cargo. DOD cargo accounted for approximately three-quarters of preference cargo in 2013. Food aid shipments have also declined. From 2005 to 2013, the amount of U.S. food aid commodities purchased and shipped from the United States by the U.S. government—and therefore subject to cargo preference—declined by 66 percent and the number of U.S.-flag vessels carrying food aid declined by more than 40 percent, from 89 to 53.[33] The number of vessels carrying food aid further declined to 38 in 2014 (see figure 4).[34]

As the number of vessels, including those carrying food aid, has declined since 2005, so has the number of mariners crewing them. MARAD estimated that in fiscal year 2005 there were at least 1,329 positions aboard 66 of the 89 vessels carrying food aid. In fiscal year 2014, the estimate was approximately 612 positions aboard 33 of 38 vessels carrying food aid.[35] Because crew members rotate over the course of a year, MARAD estimates that each position generates approximately two mariner jobs per year.[36] Using MARAD's estimating procedures, CPFA, therefore, could have supported 1,224 mariner jobs during fiscal year 2014. See figure 5 for sealift capabilities supported by CPFA.

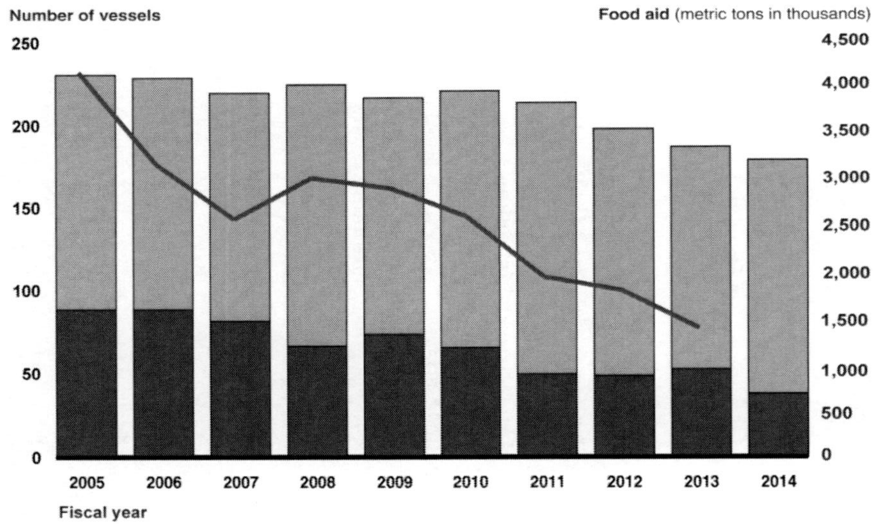

	2005	2006	2007	2008	2009	2010	2011	2012	2013	2014
Number of vessels that did not transport food aid[a]	142	140	138	158	143	155	164	149	134	141
Number of vessels that transported food aid	89	89	82	67	74	66	50	49	53	38
Food aid commodities[b]	4,062	3,081	2,510	2,938	2,832	2,541	1,901	1,759	1,362	

Source: GAO analysis of the Maritime Administration, U.S. Department of Agriculture and U.S. Agency for International Development data. | GAO-15-666

[a] Includes privately owned ocean going self-propelled vessels of 1,000 gross tons and greater.

[b] Data on food aid commodities shipped was not available for 2014.

Figure 4. U.S.-Flag Vessels and Food Aid Commodities, 2005 through 2014.

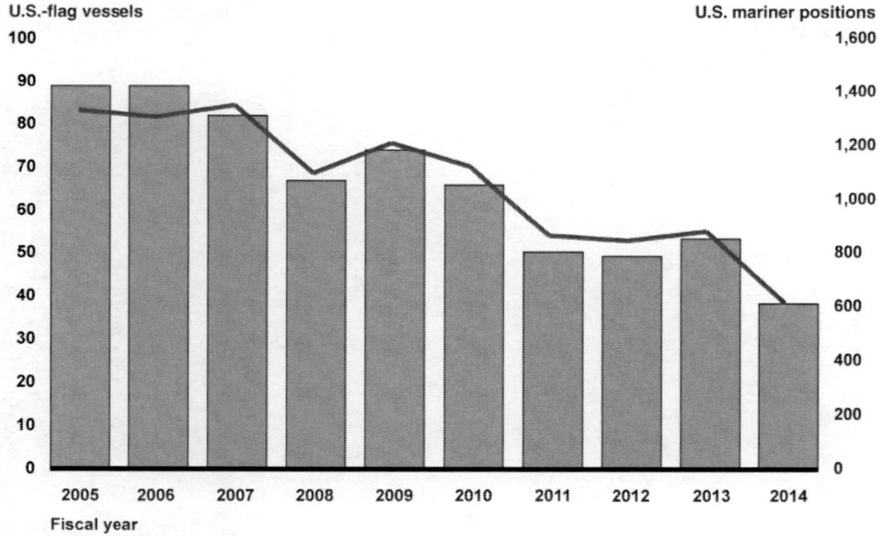

	2005	2006	2007	2008	2009	2010	2011	2012	2013	2014
U.S.-flag vessels transporting food aid	89	89	82	67	74	66	50	49	53	38
U.S. mariner positions aboard vessels transporting food aid	1,329	1,304	1,348	1,096	1,207	1,120	862	842	877	612

Source: Maritime Administration. | GAO-15-666

Note: Available positions only for oceangoing vessels with gross tonnage greater than 1,600 gross tons. Does not include positions available in tug and barge combinations, or vessels for which MARAD has no data.

Figure 5. Sealift Capabilities Supported by CPFA, 2005 through 2014.

CPFA supports some sealift capability by ensuring that a portion of U.S.-flag vessels carry some food aid cargo. We found that without CPFA, most food aid cargo would not be transported on U.S.-flag vessels. USAID and USDA review and approve contracts to ocean carriers based on CPFA requirements and lowest landed costs for the combination of necessary commodities and transportation costs. We found that if CPFA requirements had not been applied, 97 percent of food aid tonnage after the CPFA change would have been awarded to foreign-flag vessels. Even with CPFA, however, the number of U.S.-flag vessels and mariners supported by CPFA has decreased, and the overall contribution of CPFA to sealift is unclear.

DOD Has Met Its Past Sealift Needs without Full Activation of the Reserve Sealift Fleet

One intended objective of CPFA is to help ensure a merchant marine—both vessels and mariners—capable of providing sealift in times of war or national emergency. For its sealift capability needs, DOD relies on commercial vessels, including those carrying food aid, and the reserve sealift fleet, which, according to DOD, have been sufficient for its past needs. During times of war or national emergency, DOD can make the decision to use commercial or government-owned sealift capacity to meet ocean transportation requirements. According to DOD officials, DOD pays the shipping costs for its cargo to those commercial vessels that provide capacity. DOD officials also told us that a vessel does not need to be deemed militarily useful to provide sealift capability, and both U.S.- and foreign-flag vessels can be used to provide sealift. As of March 2015, there were 167 oceangoing U.S.-flag vessels that could provide sealift for DOD's needs.[37] However, vessels that participate in VISA would be afforded the first opportunity to provide sealift capabilities, as they have agreed to provide DOD with assured access to sealift capacity.[38] In March 2015, 99 oceangoing U.S.-flag vessels were enrolled in VISA, 58 of which are MSP vessels that receive a $3.1 million annual payment to support DOD in addition to any shipping costs DOD provides for its cargo. In the event provided capacity does not meet DOD's needs, DOD will activate the VISA to require additional vessel capacity be made available, as necessary.[39] DOD can also activate the reserve sealift fleet when commercial vessels cannot satisfy military operational requirements, among other reasons. The reserve sealift fleet is composed of 61 vessels, 46 of which are MARAD-owned and form part of the Ready Reserve Force and 15 DOD-owned vessels in the Military Sealift Command's Surge Sealift program.[40] See figure 6 for the composition of oceangoing U.S.-flag and the reserve sealift fleet.

DOD has never activated VISA or the entire reserve sealift fleet to meet sealift capacity needs. DOD requires access to sufficient U.S.-flag capacity to meet the most serious scenario and, according to DOD officials, available vessel capacity—U.S.- and foreign-flag—has historically been sufficient to meet DOD's needs. While VISA participants have provided sealift capacity for DOD, since the program's inception in 1997, the VISA program has never been activated. Partial activations of the reserve sealift fleet have been needed to support DOD. For example, according to the Military Sealift Command, in fiscal year 2014, 2 Ready Reserve Force vessels were activated, 1 to support the destruction of Syrian chemical weapon components in the Mediterranean, and another to support a cargo mission for U.S. Central Command; furthermore, 4 of the Military Sealift Command's Surge Sealift Program vessels were activated to support Navy exercises. According to DOD officials, only during a significant contingency would the entire reserve sealift fleet be activated, and only in the most serious scenario would the entire reserve sealift fleet be activated for a prolonged period of time, in addition to the use of commercial vessels. However, in the past 13 years, including during Operation Iraqi Freedom and Operation Enduring Freedom in Afghanistan, there has never been a time when the entire reserve sealift fleet has had to be activated. Figure 7 shows the number of Ready Reserve Force vessels, a subset of 46 vessels in the reserve sealift fleet, and mariners used for its activation since 2002.

The Number of U.S. Mariners Qualified and Available to Serve DOD's Needs under a Full and Prolonged Activation Is Uncertain

Estimated Number of Mariners Needed

MARAD has estimated the number of mariners required to fully crew both the reserve sealift fleet and commercial operations for shorter- and longer-duration surge scenarios as required by DOD.[41] DOD's most serious scenario envisions a full activation of the entire reserve sealift fleet for an extended period of time. In addition, DOD would require the use of some commercial sealift for sustainment purposes. According to MARAD, an activation of the entire reserve sealift fleet would require a total crew of 1,943 mariners for a 6-month period. However, these vessels maintain a smaller crew at all times; therefore, full activation of the fleet would require finding mariners to complete the necessary crewing levels. For example, in June 2015, there were 645 mariners already serving aboard the fleet, and thus initially activating the full fleet would require an additional 1,298 mariners. If the full fleet is activated for a period longer than 6 months, then the crew would need to be rotated and 1,943 additional mariners would be needed to fill all the positions. Using MARAD's estimates, the crew to sustain the reserve sealift fleet for 12 months would require 3,886 mariners. In addition, according to MARAD, U.S. mariners are also needed to crew commercial vessels during that same time period, including those providing sealift to DOD. MARAD officials expect all commercial vessels to continue operations during the same period during which the reserve surge fleet is activated and estimated that 9,148 mariners would be needed to crew such vessels.[42] While MARAD estimates that 3,886 mariners are needed to sustain the reserve sealift fleet, it estimates that a total of 13,034 mariners is required to both support the prolonged operation of the entire reserve sealift fleet as well as the operation of commercial vessels during a scenario requiring the prolonged full activation of the reserve sealift fleet.[43]

The Number of Mariners Available Is Uncertain

While USCG maintains data on mariner qualifications, the number of mariners potentially available—both actively sailing and willing—to operate the reserve sealift fleet under a full and prolonged activation is uncertain.

- *Number of mariners potentially qualified.* USCG data show that the number of mariners potentially qualified to operate the reserve sealift fleet has increased since fiscal year 2008. According to MARAD, the ability to crew and operate the reserve sealift fleet to meet military sealift requirements depends on having sufficient qualified mariners available in time of national emergency.[44] Mariners with such qualifications have taken specific DOD- approved training required to crew vessels in the reserve sealift fleet, according to DOD officials. The pool of mariners able to crew and operate the reserve sealift fleet includes those who have obtained their STCW and unlimited tonnage/horsepower endorsements, according to MARAD. USCG data show that from fiscal years 2008 to 2014, the number of mariners with STCW and unlimited tonnage and horsepower endorsements increased from 37,702 to 54,953 (see figure 8) [45]

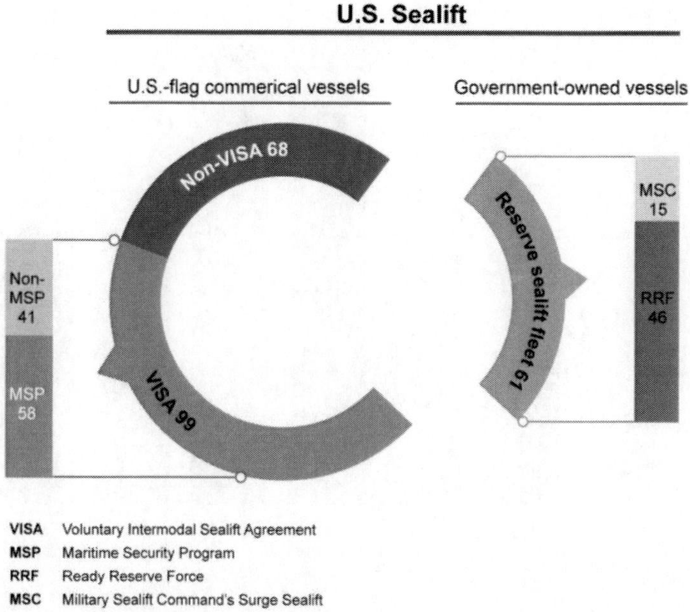

Source: Maritime Administration. | GAO-15-666

Figure 6. U.S.-Flag Commercial Vessels and the Reserve Sealift Fleet.

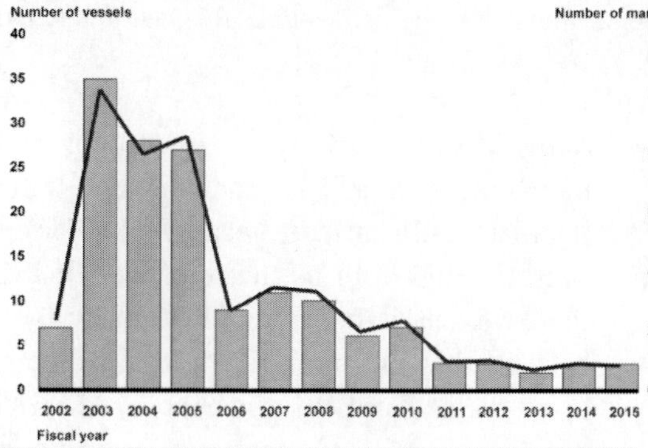

	2002	2003	2004	2005	2006	2007	2008	2009	2010	2011	2012	2013	2014	2015
Ready Reserve Force vessels activated	7	35	28	27	9	11	10	6	7	3	3	2	3	3
Mariners required to crew activated Ready Reserve Force vessles	233	1,012	792	854	266	345	332	196	233	96	99	68	89	83

Source: Maritime Administration. | GAO-15-666

Note: Only long-term exercise or contingency activations are included. Activation for routine shipyard periods, hurricane avoidance, or sea trials is not included.

Figure 7. Ready Reserve Force Vessels Activated to Provide Sealift Capabilities and Number of Mariners Required to Crew Them, 2002 through 2015.

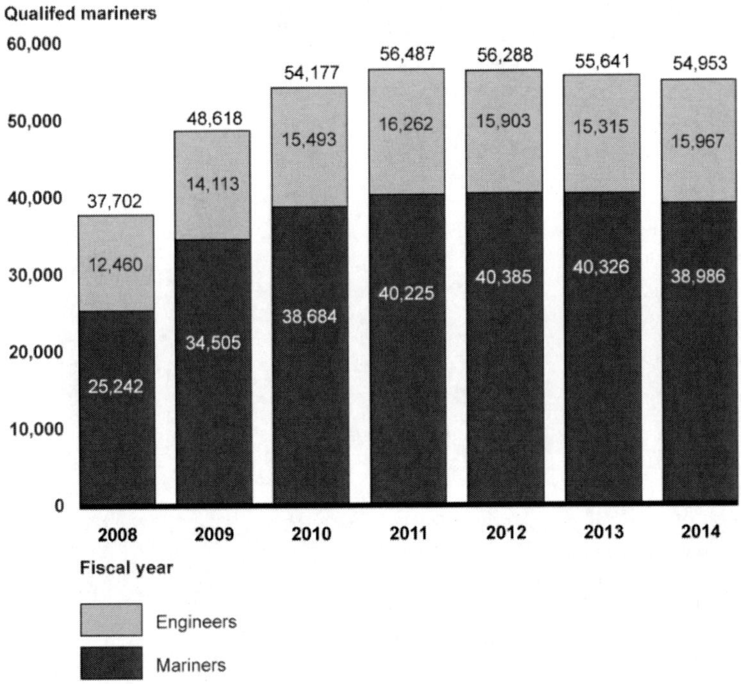

Source: U.S. Coast Guard. | GAO-15-666

Figure 8. Number of Mariners Potentially Qualified to Operate the Reserve Fleet, Fiscal Years 2008 through 2014.

- *Actively sailing mariners.* According to MARAD officials, not all mariners with STCW endorsement utilize their credential to sail internationally, in part because of a lack of jobs aboard oceangoing vessels. They told us that the pool of mariners available to operate these vessels is better represented by those who are actively sailing because they are more likely to have their training and qualifications up to date.[46] Further, according to MARAD, when U.S. mariners are not actively sailing, they typically do not maintain their memberships in the U.S. maritime labor unions, which have collective bargaining agreements for crewing the reserve sealift fleet.[47] However, complete, detailed data on actively sailing U.S. mariners are not available. USCG maintains a database on U.S. mariners and their credentials, but USCG officials noted that USCG's ability to identify actively sailing mariners is limited to the extent to which companies notify USCG of mariners sailing internationally through discharge certificate records.[48] When vessels return from an international voyage, the vessel owner is required to provide discharge certificates for all the mariners aboard to USCG, upon request. As of June 2, 2015, USCG reported that it had received 16,637 certificates of discharge for mariners with STCW and unlimited tonnage/horsepower endorsements that had sailed in the previous 18 months. However, USCG officials estimate that they do not receive all the certificates of discharge, and the number of actively sailing mariners may be higher than this.

- *Mariners who are willing.* MARAD officials noted crewing of the reserve sealift vessels is done through a voluntary system, and the number of those who would actually crew these vessels is uncertain. MARAD officials explained that the majority of mariners hold permanent positions aboard a given commercial vessel and volunteering for prolonged employment aboard the reserve sealift fleet would, in most cases, mean that they would forfeit their permanent positions. The mariners would then have to compete for a new commercial position once they finished their time in the reserve sealift fleet, a contingency that would likely decrease their likelihood of volunteering. MARAD developed the Mariner Outreach System (MOS) to monitor, among other things, U.S. mariners' willingness to crew the reserve sealift fleet. U.S. mariners have the option to consent to be contacted in the event of a national emergency or sealift crisis through the USCG application for merchant mariner credential or the MOS. From 2008 to 2014, about 9,000 mariners, on average annually, have consented to be contacted through the USCG application for merchant mariner credential process every year. For example, during fiscal year 2014, 9,682 U.S. mariners consented to allow MARAD to contact them. While these mariners consent to be contacted, they are not obligated to sail. At the same time, they have shown some willingness to crew the reserve sealift fleet. However, MARAD officials noted that not all of the mariners in MOS have the endorsements and training required to crew vessels in the reserve sealift fleet.
- *Strategic Sealift Officers.* In addition to the pool of mariners who could volunteer to support the reserve sealift fleet, Strategic Sealift Officers can be called to duty to fill officer positions aboard the reserve sealift fleet if a shortage of qualified civilian mariners exists. According to a DOD official, as of April 2015, the Strategic Sealift

Officer program consisted of 1,973 officers, of whom 1,063 were not actively sailing. However, DOD officials told us, to date, merchant mariners have been sufficient to support sealift capabilities and Strategic Sealift Officers have never been called into duty to crew the reserve sealift fleet.

MARAD Has Not Fully Assessed the Sufficiency of Mariners Available under DOD's Most Serious Scenario

While the USCG database shows over 16,000 potentially qualified and actively sailing mariners, MARAD stated that not all these mariners would be readily available to crew the reserve sealift fleet and maintain ocean commercial operations. As of May 2015, MARAD has estimated that 11,280 U.S. mariners were readily available based on its assumptions and analysis of USCG data.[49] According to MARAD officials, this number is sufficient to support the initial activation of the reserve sealift fleet for 6 months but insufficient to support the prolonged operations of all the vessels, after the initial crew is rotated. MARAD concluded that at least 1,378 more mariners would need to be available to meet the needs of the prolonged operation of the entire reserve sealift fleet as well as the operation of commercial vessels.[50] According to MARAD officials, they expect the shortage to occur for senior officer positions but not at the lower officer positions, such as third mate or third assistant engineer, since the merchant marine academies graduate their students each year with these ranks. MARAD officials acknowledged that there are more mariners qualified to support the operation of the reserve sealift fleet but stated that they may not be available to do so in part because of either their current location or employment, or lack of appropriate experience for a particular officer position. However, MARAD did not reassess the sufficiency of the mariner pool using different assumptions to include a bigger portion of those qualified, such as the more than 1,000 Strategic Sealift Officers who were not actively sailing as of April 2015, or consider mechanisms to reach out to the mariners it excluded in its analysis if there was a full, prolonged activation of the reserve sealift fleet. Figure 9 summarizes the potential mariner supply for a prolonged surge based on USCG data on potentially qualified actively sailing mariners and MARAD's estimates on those readily available.

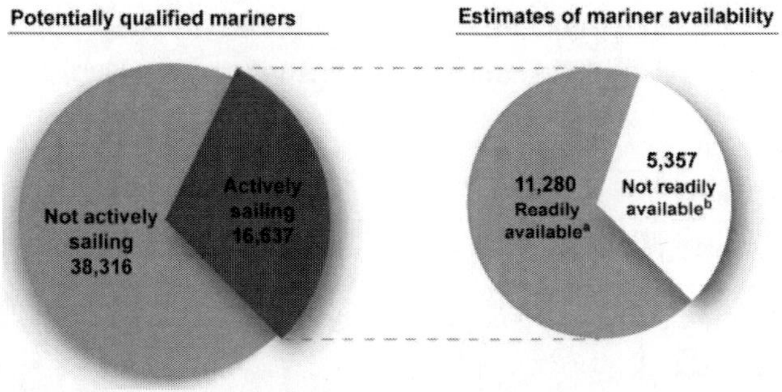

Source: U.S. Coast Guard and MARAD (data). | GAO-15-666

Notes: The data on potentially qualified mariners, including engineers, who are not actively sailing comes from the U.S. Coast Guard's Merchant Mariner Licensing and Documentation System as of April 2015.

[a] The estimate of qualified mariners, including engineers, who are readily available is MARAD's estimate as of October 2014, based on USCG's data at the time and its own assumptions.

[b] The estimate of qualified mariners, including engineers, who are not readily available, is GAO's calculation, based on USCG's data and MARAD's estimate.

Figure 9. Potential Mariner Supply for a Prolonged Surge, Fiscal Year 2015.

SELECTED STAKEHOLDERS HAVE DIFFERING VIEWS ON OPTIONS TO IMPROVE THE SUSTAINABILITY OF THE OCEANGOING U.S.- FLAG FLEET

Given that the number of U.S.-flag vessels has declined since fiscal year 2005, we interviewed 29 stakeholders knowledgeable about CPFA to obtain their views on what policy options, if any, could improve the sustainability of the oceangoing U.S.-flag fleet, including those carrying food aid.[51] The 29 stakeholders we interviewed suggested 27 unique options; 18 of these stakeholders subsequently selected what they believe to be the top 3 options from among those suggested as well as provided comments on a variety of the options. The 27 options ranged from increasing the CPFA minimum requirement from 50 to 100 percent to eliminating CPFA altogether, with the stakeholders' relationships to the maritime industry highly related to the nature of their selection. Results from stakeholders overall, maritime industry stakeholders, and other maritime stakeholders are presented in the figure below.[52] (See app. IV for a complete list of options and counts—both overall and broken out by stakeholder category.)

Figure 10 lists the frequently selected options by stakeholders overall, maritime industry stakeholders, and other maritime stakeholders.[53]

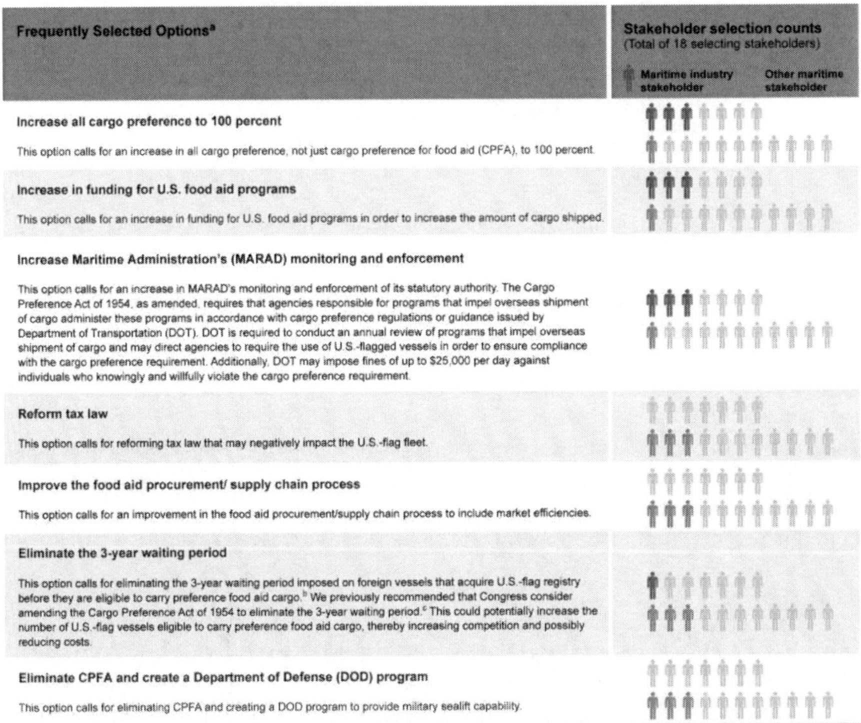

Frequently Selected Options[a]	Stakeholder selection counts (Total of 18 selecting stakeholders) Maritime industry stakeholder / Other maritime stakeholder
Increase all cargo preference to 100 percent This option calls for an increase in all cargo preference, not just cargo preference for food aid (CPFA), to 100 percent.	
Increase in funding for U.S. food aid programs This option calls for an increase in funding for U.S. food aid programs in order to increase the amount of cargo shipped.	
Increase Maritime Administration's (MARAD) monitoring and enforcement This option calls for an increase in MARAD's monitoring and enforcement of its statutory authority. The Cargo Preference Act of 1954, as amended, requires that agencies responsible for programs that impel overseas shipment of cargo administer these programs in accordance with cargo preference regulations or guidance issued by Department of Transportation (DOT). DOT is required to conduct an annual review of programs that impel overseas shipment of cargo and may direct agencies to require the use of U.S.-flagged vessels in order to ensure compliance with the cargo preference requirement. Additionally, DOT may impose fines of up to $25,000 per day against individuals who knowingly and willfully violate the cargo preference requirement.	
Reform tax law This option calls for reforming tax law that may negatively impact the U.S.-flag fleet.	
Improve the food aid procurement/ supply chain process This option calls for an improvement in the food aid procurement/supply chain process to include market efficiencies.	
Eliminate the 3-year waiting period This option calls for eliminating the 3-year waiting period imposed on foreign vessels that acquire U.S.-flag registry before they are eligible to carry preference food aid cargo.[b] We previously recommended that Congress consider amending the Cargo Preference Act of 1954 to eliminate the 3-year waiting period.[c] This could potentially increase the number of U.S.-flag vessels eligible to carry preference food aid cargo, thereby increasing competition and possibly reducing costs.	
Eliminate CPFA and create a Department of Defense (DOD) program This option calls for eliminating CPFA and creating a DOD program to provide military sealift capability.	

Source : GAO analysis of stakeholder selections. | GAO-15-666

[a] The frequently selected options are those options that were selected by 4 or more of the 18 stakeholders or 3 or more maritime industry stakeholders or other maritime stakeholders. They are listed in this table in no particular order.

[b] *See* 46 U.S.C. § 55305(a). The 3-year wait provision from the Cargo Preference Act of 1954 does not apply to the 60 vessels enrolled in the Maritime Security Program. Foreign-built vessels are eligible to carry military preference cargo as well as Export-Import Bank financed cargo immediately upon registering under the U.S.-flag. 46 U.S.C. § 53102(b).

[c] GAO, International Food Assistance: Funding Development Projects through the Purchase, Shipment, and Sale of U.S. Commodities Is Inefficient and Can Cause Adverse Market Impacts, GAO-11-636 (Washington, D.C.: June 23, 2011).

Figure 10. Frequently Selected Options to Improve the Sustainability of the Oceangoing U.S.-Flag Fleet, Including Vessels Carrying Food Aid.

Stakeholders' Selections

Stakeholders. The options that 4 of the 18 stakeholders who selected what they believe to be the top 3 options from among those suggested were to increase cargo preference on all government cargo to 100 percent; increase funding for U.S. food aid programs; increase MARAD's monitoring and enforcement of its statutory authority, and eliminate the 3- year waiting period imposed on foreign vessels that acquire U.S.-flag registry before they are eligible to carry preference food aid cargo.[54]

In addition, there were a number of options that 3 of the 18 stakeholders selected, including reforming tax law that may negatively affect the U.S.- flag fleet, improving the food aid procurement/ supply chain process to include market efficiencies, eliminating CPFA and creating a DOD program to provide military sealift capability, increasing the CPFA minimum requirement from 50 to 75 percent, increasing the CPFA minimum requirement from 50 to 100 percent, reinstating OFD and TPEF reimbursements, subsidizing U.S.-flag fleet vessels, and reforming tort law that may negatively affect the U.S.-flag fleet.

Maritime industry stakeholders. The options that 3 of the 7 maritime industry stakeholders selected as being among their top 3 were to increase all cargo preference to 100 percent, increase funding for U.S. food aid programs, and increase MARAD's monitoring and enforcement of its statutory authority.[55] All 3 of these options were also options that the 18 stakeholders frequently selected, but all 3 options are different from the options that the 11 other maritime industry stakeholders frequently selected. Furthermore, support for these 3 options varied within this category of maritime industry stakeholders. For example, while some maritime industry stakeholders selected a particular option, others commented on the possible negative effects of the same option.

In addition, there were 2 options that 2 of the 7 maritime industry stakeholders selected: increasing the CPFA minimum requirement from 50 to 100 percent and enforcing cargo preference requirements for all U.S. government agencies.

Other maritime stakeholders. The options that 3 of the 11 other maritime stakeholders selected as being among their top 3 were to reform tax law that may negatively affect the U.S.-flag fleet, improve the food aid procurement/supply chain process to include market efficiencies, eliminate the 3-year waiting period imposed on foreign vessels that acquire U.S.-flag registry before they are eligible to carry preference food aid cargo, and eliminate CPFA and create a DOD program to provide military sealift capability.[56] The option to eliminate the 3-year waiting period was also frequently selected by the 18 stakeholders, but all four options are different from the options frequently selected by the 7 maritime industry stakeholders. Furthermore, support for these 4 options varied within this category of other maritime stakeholders.

In addition, there were a number of options that 2 of the 11 other maritime stakeholders selected, including increasing the CPFA minimum requirement from 50 to 75 percent, reinstating the OFD and TPEF reimbursements, determining the minimum number of vessels and mariners needed to sustain the U.S.-flag fleet, subsidizing U.S.-flag fleet vessels, reforming tort law that may negatively affect the U.S.-flag fleet, and not requiring CPFA compliance by country.

Stakeholders' and Agency Officials' Comments

When selecting their top three options, stakeholders also provided comments on any options, and agency officials later provided comments on the options frequently selected by stakeholders. These comments are summarized below for each of the frequently selected options.

Increase All Cargo Preference to 100 Percent

- Stakeholders from both categories provided comments both supporting and opposing increasing all cargo preference to 100 percent. For example, 1 maritime industry stakeholder commented that an increase could help the U.S. government maintain a strong U.S.-flag fleet, while another commented that too much food aid funding would be lost to U.S.-flag rates, which are generally higher than foreign-flag rates. Similarly, 1 other maritime stakeholder commented that an increase to 100 percent would be preferable, while another commented that the U.S. government should not give carriers with U.S-flag vessels a monopoly and believed these carriers would keep raising their shipping rates. Comments from maritime industry stakeholders were mixed, with 3 supporting the option and 2 not supporting the option. On one hand, 1 maritime industry stakeholder expressed support for the increase as a means of redressing the decline in U.S. government cargo shipped. On the other hand, another maritime industry stakeholder commented that only negative effects were associated with this option. For example, too much food aid funding would be lost to higher shipping rates.

- According to USAID and USDA officials, there are no potential benefits and only potential negative effects associated with increasing all cargo preference to 100 percent. USAID officials believe that this option would not be beneficial to U.S. food aid programs. According to USAID officials, the potential negative effects would be that with increased cargo preference requirements, food aid programs would experience greater transportation costs and significantly less flexibility in determining the shipping process. USAID officials said that this option would negatively affect the food aid program's size, and ultimately the programs would ship fewer commodities to fewer places and reach fewer beneficiaries. According to USAID officials, the U.S. government could implement the option of increasing all cargo preference to 100 percent only through a change in the cargo preference statute. According to USDA officials, one of the potential negative effects of increasing all cargo preference to 100 percent is that, with USDA food assistance constrained by the amount of money budgeted for each program, increasing cargo preference to 100 percent would limit the number of shipments because of the higher cost of shipping on U.S.-flag vessels. In addition, there are a limited number of U.S.-flag vessels that participate in food aid shipments and lack of availability of U.S.- flag vessels could cause delays in shipments, breaks in food aid pipelines, and disruption of programs on the ground.

Increase Funding for U.S. Food Aid Programs

- Stakeholders from both categories provided comments supporting increasing funding for U.S. food aid programs, and no stakeholders provided opposing comments. Furthermore, stakeholders commented that funding has decreased despite factors such as higher costs and greater food aid needs. For example, 1 maritime industry stakeholder commented that funding for U.S. international food aid programs is currently inadequate, as it has been cut significantly in recent years while certain costs have risen. Similarly, 1 other maritime stakeholder commented that funding has gone down sharply in inflation-adjusted terms over the past years even as the number of disaster-affected peoples worldwide has grown. Maritime industry stakeholders who commented on this option were all in support of it. One maritime industry stakeholder emphasized the multiple interests these programs support, including those of DOD and the U.S. agricultural business. The stakeholder also commented that the programs demonstrate the country's commitment to helping those in need and supporting foreign policy goals.

- According to USAID and USDA officials, there are no potential negative effects and only potential benefits of increasing funding for U.S. food aid programs. According to USAID officials, the potential benefit of increasing funding would be that, along with refinements made to cargo preference regulations, more recipients would be reached. However, USAID officials explained that it is difficult to quantify any effect on the U.S.-flag fleet. USAID officials stated they would continue to program food assistance resources in the most appropriate modality for the response, and comply with all applicable legislative parameters. According to USAID officials, the U.S. government could implement the option of increasing funding for U.S. food aid programs through the congressional budget process. According to USDA officials, a potential benefit of increasing funding is that, with the Food for Progress program currently limited because of a $40 million cap on transportation costs, it is difficult to meet the legislated minimum tonnage requirement for the program.[57] The high shipping rates absorbed by the food assistance programs often result in fewer agreements and shipments in any given fiscal year. Any increase in funding for the program would have to be in the form of an increase to the transportation cap to have an impact on the program. USDA officials added that increasing funding for U.S. food aid programs could help to improve the sustainability of the oceangoing U.S.-flag fleet because increased funding would result in increased shipments of food aid, and increased shipments would benefit the U.S.-flag fleet.

Increase MARAD's Monitoring and Enforcement

- Stakeholders from both categories provided comments both supporting and opposing increasing MARAD's monitoring and enforcement of its statutory authority. Maritime industry stakeholders who commented on this option were all in support of it. Two maritime industry stakeholders commented that MARAD has not completed the rulemaking process, with one questioning why it has not been done and the other citing the necessity of doing it.[58]

- According to USAID and USDA officials, there are no potential benefits and only potential negative effects associated with increasing MARAD's monitoring and enforcement of its statutory authority. According to USAID officials, the potential negative effects would be a loss of time, control, and flexibility in implementing food aid programs. This ultimately would result in less efficient, less timely programming and distribution, and costs to programs. According to USAID officials, the U.S. government could implement the option of increasing MARAD's monitoring and enforcement through the interagency rulemaking process. According to USDA officials, a potential negative effect is that it would potentially reduce the role of programming agencies with regard to cargo preference. They said that MARAD likely does not have a complete and thorough understanding of food aid regulations and policies. USDA has consistently maintained compliance with cargo preference and sees no benefit to having MARAD's increased involvement in monitoring and enforcement.

Reform Tax Law

- Only 1 other maritime stakeholder provided a comment either supporting or opposing reforming tax law. The single comment was in support of the option, stating that it would be particularly helpful to the international competitiveness of the U.S.-flag fleet. However, 1 maritime industry stakeholder commented that the tonnage tax regime works very well today as long as it is interpreted correctly. Another maritime industry stakeholder stated that U.S. tax law currently alleviates some of the burden of federal income taxes on U.S. vessel owners (although tonnage tax could be improved and U.S. vessel owners remain subject to state, local, and other taxes), but provides no tax relief for U.S. merchant mariners serving on vessels internationally, in contrast to merchant mariners serving on foreign vessels, who generally pay no taxes to any jurisdiction.
- No agency officials commented on the option of reforming tax law.

Improve the Food Aid Procurement/Supply Chain Process

- Stakeholders from both categories provided comments generally supporting improving the food aid procurement/supply chain process. For example, other maritime stakeholders who commented on this option were generally in support of it. One stakeholder commented that there are a variety of ways to improve the process and the options need to be discussed with all parties—implementing agencies, commodity and food product vendors, freight forwarders, shipping companies, labor, and U.S. government agencies—to find the best solutions.
- According to USAID officials, the potential benefits of improving the food aid procurement/supply chain process to include market efficiencies would be that some cost savings would result from more effective implementation of commercial terms and practices. However, USAID officials anticipate that improving the food aid procurement/supply chain process would have an insignificant effect on improving the sustainability of the oceangoing U.S.-flag fleet unless the barriers to entry were lowered. According to USAID officials, the U.S. government could implement this option at the USAID program and contract levels. USDA officials stated that they welcome improvements to the food aid procurement/supply chain process. However, USDA officials noted that USDA is required to follow the Federal Acquisition Regulation for procurement.

Eliminate the Three-Year Waiting Period

- Other maritime stakeholders who provided comments on the option of eliminating the 3-year waiting period on foreign vessels that acquire U.S.-flag registry before they are eligible to carry preference food aid cargo generally believed that it would remove a bureaucratic obstacle and could lead to increased competition. However, several maritime industry stakeholders commented that the elimination could lead to vessels flagging in and out of the U.S.-flag fleet whenever convenient. While stakeholders who commented on this option generally supported it, 1 questioned why the period could not be shortened to 1 year.
- Both USAID and USDA officials generally provided comments supporting eliminating the 3-year waiting period and both commented

that a change to current cargo preference statute would be required to do so. According to USAID officials, eliminating the 3-year waiting period could lower freight rates. It also could increase competition and eliminate any existing monopolies.[59] There is a very small pool of U.S.-flag vessel owners who are eligible to participate in the carriage of agricultural food aid commodities. This limits agencies' selection and flexibility, and leads to inefficient choices of trade that do not conform to commercial practices, such as with combination voyages to ports in Southwest Africa, East Africa, and Southeast Asia. According to USAID officials, eliminating the 3-year waiting period could help to improve the sustainability of the oceangoing U.S.-flag fleet by lowering foreign-flag vessels' entry barriers, and growing the U.S.-flag fleet. According to USDA officials, more vessels participating as U.S-flag vessels would increase competition and potentially reduce shipping rates. According to USDA officials, to avoid the potential negative effects of eliminating the waiting period, there would need to be some sort of vetting period to ensure that foreign vessels that have acquired U.S.-flag registry are indeed equipped to move food aid cargo. According to USDA officials, eliminating the waiting period could also help to improve the sustainability of the oceangoing U.S.-flag fleet because vessels that have transitioned from foreign to U.S.- flag may be younger and in better condition than some U.S.-flag vessels currently participating in the food aid shipments. MARAD officials explained that there is a cost to flag in and out of the U.S.- flag fleet.[60]

Eliminate CPFA and Create a DOD Program

- Stakeholders from both categories provided comments both supporting and opposing eliminating CPFA and creating a DOD program to provide military sealift capability. Comments from other maritime stakeholders on this option were evenly split. Specifically, 1 stakeholder commented that this was the best idea of all the options, separating food aid from military readiness, while another stakeholder commented that this would be more costly.
- USAID officials cited potential benefits of eliminating CPFA, and USDA cited both potential benefits and negative effects with this option. According to USAID officials, the potential benefits would be increased flexibility and significant cost savings to the food aid

programs. According to USDA officials, the potential benefits would be that competition would increase, U.S.-flag rates would theoretically be lower, and a large number of foreign-flag vessels could participate. The expected reduction in shipping rates would result in an increase to the number of food assistance agreements under the Food for Progress program. Eliminating CPFA would greatly benefit the food assistance programs. According to USDA officials, the potential negative effects of eliminating CPFA and creating a DOD program would be that those U.S.-flag steamship companies that rely on revenue from food aid shipments may suffer financially. In addition, the unfamiliarity of foreign-flag vessels with food aid shipments could be problematic.

CONCLUSIONS

U.S. food aid programs play an important role in improving food security and alleviating hunger for millions of people around the world. How well USAID and USDA can achieve food aid programs' goals depends on the effective and efficient use of food aid resources. The elimination of reimbursements to USAID and USDA, which the agencies used to fund food aid programs, further accentuates the importance of effectively using their limited food aid resources for the programs' goals. Under U.S. law, a minimum proportion of U.S. food aid must be shipped on U.S.-flag vessels to promote both national security and commercial interests. However, because using U.S.-flag vessels is often more expensive than using foreign-flag vessels, a larger portion of the food aid budget must go to shipping costs than if there were no such requirement. Changes in the law in 2012 reduced the U.S.-flag minimum requirement for food assistance from 75 to 50 percent, decreasing the overall shipping cost of food aid, especially for programs administered by USAID. However, USDA has experienced limited savings, because the agency is subject to a court order requiring it to administer cargo preference on a country-by-country basis; USDA's utilization of foreign-flag vessels was far below the 50 percent allowed by the 2012 law. GAO has twice recommended that key agencies administering CPFA agree on a consistent interpretation of CPFA requirements through an MOU, but the agencies have only addressed the definition of vessel categories and not the definition of "geographic area." As USDA continues to use a more stringent definition of geographic area when implementing CPFA, it is not able to take advantage of the shipping price decreases that USAID utilizes. Pursuant to the terms of the court order requiring USDA to comply with CPFA on a country-by-country basis, an MOU embodying an agreement between USDA and MARAD on a consistent definition of "geographic area" would allow USDA to administer CPFA using a method other than country-by- country.

CPFA ensures that U.S.-flag vessels carry a portion of food aid, but the extent to which CPFA contributes to sufficient sealift capabilities for DOD is unclear. While DOD officials noted that the number of U.S.-flag vessels is sufficient for contingency needs including a full and prolonged activation of the reserve fleet, it is unclear whether there are enough mariners available to fulfill this scenario, particularly in senior officer positions. MARAD has estimated that there is a shortage of qualified mariners available to address a full and prolonged activation of the reserve fleet. However, its estimate does not fully account for all of the potential sources of supply, including reserve naval officers. Without a full understanding of both the need for and potential available supply of mariners under DOD's most serious scenario, the U.S. government is limited in its capacity to address any potential imbalance. Furthermore, the U.S. government cannot guarantee that the use of food aid programming funds to pay higher U.S.-flag shipping prices under CPFA is achieving the intended goal of maintaining a merchant marine capable of providing sealift capability in time of war or national emergency.

Matter for Congressional Consideration

While recognizing that cargo preference serves policy goals established by Congress with respect to the U.S. merchant marine, including maintenance of a fleet capable of serving as a naval and military auxiliary in time of war or national emergency, Congress should consider clarifying cargo preference legislation regarding the definition of "geographic area" to ensure that agencies can fully utilize the flexibility Congress granted to them when it lowered the CPFA requirement.

Recommendation for Executive Action

GAO recommends that the Secretary of Transportation direct the Administrator of MARAD to study the potential availability of all qualified mariners needed to meet a full and prolonged activation of the reserve sealift fleet. In the study, MARAD should identify potential solutions to address the mariner shortfall if one is still identified.

AGENCY COMMENTS AND OUR EVALUATION

We provided a draft copy of this report to DOT, USDA, USAID, DOD, and USCG for their review and comments. In its written comments, DOT concurred with our recommendation to study the potential availability of all qualified mariners needed to meet a full and prolonged activation of the reserve sealift fleet. DOT stated that MARAD has been reviewing the adequacy of existing plans to recruit mariner volunteers to crew the full reserve fleet. Furthermore, DOT noted that 13,000 mariners are required to crew all the vessels in the fleet for sustained operations. During the course of our review, MARAD provided the estimated number of mariners required for prolonged full activation as 12,658. When we followed up on the number given in DOT's written comments, however, DOT noted that the estimated number was 13,034 instead. While MARAD officials outlined some factors and high-level calculations they utilize when computing such an estimate, we could not assess the reliability or accuracy of either estimate because MARAD did not have a final report that documented and presented precise calculations and methods that they used. We therefore were unable to verify the details of their estimates. We noted MARAD's different estimated numbers of mariners in our report. We also received agencies' technical comments, which we incorporated where appropriate.

Thomas Melito
Director, International Affairs and Trade

APPENDIX I: SCOPE AND METHODOLOGY

This report examines (1) cargo preference for food aid's (CPFA) impact on food aid shipping cost and U.S. agencies' implementation of CPFA requirements, (2) the extent to which the implementation of CPFA requirements contributes to sufficient sealift capacity, and (3) stakeholder views on options to improve the sustainability of the oceangoing U.S.-flag fleet.[61]

To address our objectives, we analyzed cargo preference legislation as well as documents, guidance, and data on CPFA provided by the U.S. Agency for International Development (USAID), the U.S. Department of Agriculture (USDA), and the Department of Transportation's (DOT) Maritime Administration (MARAD). We also interviewed USAID, USDA, and MARAD officials about each agency's role and responsibilities regarding CPFA, the processes each agency uses to implement CPFA, the cost implications of such requirements on food aid programs, and the impact of such requirements on cargo preference objectives.[62]

To determine the CPFA requirements' impact on food aid shipping cost, we analyzed food aid procurement data for both USAID and USDA from April 2011 through fiscal year 2014, including some bulk food commodities and all packaged food commodities and shipment data for April 2011 through fiscal year 2014.[63] With the exception of the detailed discussion in appendix II, we use the term "solicitation" to mean solicitation line. Each agency announces solicitations for bids to ship food aid. Each solicitation includes a line for a specific amount of a specific commodity to be procured for a specific food aid program. For example, a recent solicitation for USAID freight included one line for 51,710 metric tons of sorghum for the World Food Program's food aid program in Sudan. During this time period, CPFA requirement levels changed from 75 to 50 percent. We examined the number of total U.S.-flag and foreign- flag bids per solicitation. We analyzed USDA and USAID bid data to estimate the cost difference between U.S.- and foreign-flag vessels and the CPFA requirements' effect on shipping awards. We used regression analysis to identify the impact of the changes in the CPFA requirements on the cost of shipping U.S. food aid. For detailed discussion of our methodology and results, see Appendix II.

To examine the extent to which the implementation of CPFA requirements contributes to sufficient sealift capacity, we reviewed the Department of Defense's (DOD) documentation related to the Voluntary Intermodal Sealift Agreement (VISA) and the Maritime Security Program (MSP) and interviewed DOD officials about the sealift capability and military usefulness of the vessels in the U.S.-flag fleet. We also analyzed MARAD's data on U.S.-flag vessels, including those carrying food aid cargo and the number of mariner positions aboard such vessels. We interviewed MARAD officials to understand the reliability of the data provided. According to MARAD officials, MARAD receives information directly from operating companies related to vessel specifications, as well as crewing requirements. Such information is stored in the Mariner Outreach System (MOS). Information stored in MOS was used to provide vessel crewing information for commercial and reserve sealift vessels. Further, MARAD officials used the Cargo Preferences Overview System, which records bills of lading, to identify those vessels carrying food aid cargo. We found the U.S.-flag vessel and mariner positions data sufficiently reliable for the purposes of this report. Furthermore, we obtained U.S. merchant mariner credential data available through the U.S. Coast Guard's (USCG) Merchant Mariner Licensing and Documentation System and interviewed USCG officials to understand the number of U.S. mariners with Standards of Training, Certification and Watchkeeping (STCW) and unlimited tonnage/horsepower endorsements. The Merchant Mariner Licensing and Documentation System stores information on merchant mariners' credentials and endorsements. We found overall credential and endorsement information to be sufficiently reliable for the purposes of this report. We also obtained data on the number of actively sailing mariners from USCG. The data received represents mariners with STCW and unlimited tonnage/horsepower endorsements for which USCG obtained discharge certificates during the last 18 months. However, according to officials we interviewed it likely underrepresents the number of mariners that sailed during this period because discharge certificates may not have been received for all mariners that have sailed. Further, USCG indicated that while it had checks in place to avoid double counting of mariners that filed multiple discharge certificates during this period, there was also a possibility of some double counting of the mariners that sailed more than once during this time period. We are presenting this number, with its limitations, to help place MARAD's estimate of the number of available mariners into some context. We also interviewed MARAD officials to understand the crewing process for the Reserve Sealift Fleet and the number of U.S. mariners available to support DOD needs in time of national emergency. MARAD officials provided an estimate of the number of available mariners. MARAD officials told us that they estimated the number of mariners needed to ensure that the entire Reserve Sealift Fleet was able to conduct prolonged operations while full commercial operations continued by calculating the number of positions on each vessel, and comparing this sum with the estimate of available mariners. During the course of our review, MARAD provided the estimated number of mariners needed as 12,658. In commenting on our draft report, however, DOT noted that the estimated number was instead 13,034. However, these estimates, as well as the estimates of the number of the available mariners, are of undetermined reliability because we were only partially able to assess them. While MARAD officials outlined the data sources and key factors they considered when making these estimates, they reported that they did not have a final report that documented and presented precise calculations and methods that they used, and we were therefore unable to examine the details of their estimates. We determined that while we could comment on MARAD's stated rationale and basic approach to estimating the sufficiency of the number of mariners, we could not assess the accuracy of MARAD's estimates on the number of mariners available or the number of mariners required. However, we are reporting this number to provide context for our findings on the data sources that MARAD used and the key factors that they considered.

To obtain stakeholder views on options to improve the sustainability of the U.S.-flag fleet, we conducted semistructured interviews and requested follow-up documentation from a nongeneralizable sample of 29 stakeholders knowledgeable about CPFA issues. We created an initial list of stakeholders using internal knowledge of CPFA. We then added more stakeholders based on interviewee responses to our question on whom else they thought we should speak with, considering, among other factors, how often others suggested we meet with them, the representation of their subcategory, and their location. For example, we conducted site visits at ports that we selected based on their ranking compared with that of other ports in terms of net commodity weight (metric tons) of food aid as well as the presence of stakeholders in the area. We categorized these stakeholders into maritime industry stakeholders—those stakeholders that self-identified as brokers, carriers, freight forwarders, and mariners—and other maritime stakeholders—those stakeholders that self-identified as academia, commodities, freight forwarders, implementing partners or nongovernmental organizations (NGO),[64] ports, and trade associations.[65]

The intent of our semistructured interviews was to have stakeholders identify any options to improve the sustainability of the oceangoing U.S.- flag fleet, including food aid–carrying U.S.-flag vessels. During these interviews, we orally explained to stakeholders that our review is focused only on the oceangoing vessels of the U.S.-flag fleet and our review is on the topic of cargo preference for food aid. Cargo preference for food aid (CPFA) is sometimes referred to as agricultural cargo preference (ACP), but for the purposes of this report, we refer to it as CPFA. We did not specifically ask stakeholders to consider the effect that options may have on food aid. We consolidated interview responses to create a comprehensive list of 27 policy options for stakeholder comment.[66] To ensure the accuracy of our consolidation effort, we internally reviewed our coding and reconciled any discrepancies.

As a follow-up to our semistructured interviews, we sent the list of 27 options to all 29 stakeholders, requesting that they select what they believe to be the top 3 options from among those suggested and provide any comments. Twenty of the 29 stakeholders we interviewed responded to this follow-up request. Eighteen of these stakeholders (7 maritime industry stakeholders and 11 other maritime stakeholders) selected what they believe to be the top 3 options from among those suggested and provided comments on a variety of the options, while 2 of these stakeholders (both other maritime stakeholders) responded that they would not provide their views because they did not favor any of the options.[67] We tallied the stakeholder follow-up responses to determine the options frequently selected by all stakeholders and maritime industry stakeholders compared with other maritime stakeholders. A complete list of all options suggested by stakeholders and how often stakeholders from the two categories of stakeholders selected each option can be found in appendix IV. In addition, we tallied the stakeholder follow-up responses to identify any overlap among selections made by the two categories of stakeholders. Our discussion of stakeholders' selected options is based on what they selected as their top 3 options. Because of this, when we report that a certain number of stakeholders selected an option, it does not necessarily mean that the remaining stakeholders did not support the given option. Rather, it means that those stakeholders did not select it as one of their top 3 options.

While we received 20 of 29 responses to our second phase of data collection on options and this set of responses is neither a complete universe of the selected stakeholders nor a sample generalizable to the full population of stakeholders, we present the results of our analysis to identify general tendencies in the policy options preferred by a set of important stakeholders knowledgeable about CPFA issues.

To obtain agency officials' views on stakeholders' suggested options, we requested officials from the Department of Defense (DOD), DOT, USDA, USAID, and USCG submit any views in writing on the options frequently selected by stakeholders.

We conducted this performance audit from October 2014 to August 2015 in accordance with generally accepted government auditing standards. Those standards require that we plan and perform the audit to obtain sufficient, appropriate evidence to provide a reasonable basis for our findings and conclusions based on our audit objectives. We believe that the evidence obtained provides a reasonable basis for our findings and conclusions based on our audit objectives.

APPENDIX II: ANALYSIS OF THE NUMBER OF OCEAN FREIGHT BIDS AND FOOD AID SHIPPING RATES

We analyzed the effect of the changes in cargo preference for food aid (CPFA) requirements in 2012 on the number of bids from ocean freight carriers and on food aid shipping rates. In July 2012, the Moving Ahead for Progress in the 21st Century Act of 2012 reduced the minimum required level of food aid to be shipped on U.S.-flag vessels from 75 to 50 percent and eliminated the Great Lakes Set-Aside, which required that at least 25 percent of Title II packaged food aid tonnage be shipped out from Great Lakes ports each month.[68] The act also eliminated the Maritime Administration's reimbursement to the U.S. Department of Agriculture (USDA) and the U.S. Agency for International Development (USAID) for the ocean freight differential resulting from the CPFA requirements.

Because the CPFA requirements require that a certain percentage of U.S. food aid be shipped on U.S.-flag vessels, some foreign-flag carriers may have been deterred from bidding on some solicitations knowing that they would be unlikely to win the shipping award.[69] This would be the case, especially when 25 percent of Title II packaged food aid tonnage was allocated to Great Lakes ports. According to a 2010 study, food aid shipped through Great Lakes ports was mostly shipped on lower-priced foreign-flag vessels because the portion allocated to the Great Lakes ports was made without consideration of the vessel's flag as mandated by Section 17 of the Maritime Security Act of 1995.[70] Most of the remaining 75 percent of Title II packaged food aid would then be required to be shipped on U.S.-flag vessels. The lower percentage required to be shipped on U.S.-flag vessels may encourage foreign-flag carriers to participate in the bidding process, especially for certain routes for which they did not previously participate. In addition, more competition and higher participation from foreign-flag carriers after the CPFA change may lead to lower overall shipping rates because foreign-flag vessels on average charge lower shipping rates. Our hypothesis is that after the relaxation of the CPFA requirements in July 2012, the number of bids from foreign-flag vessels would increase and overall food aid shipping rates would decrease.

We developed statistical models to assess the effect of the July 2012 changes in the CPFA requirements, after controlling for a variety of factors that may affect the number of bids received for each solicitation and food aid shipping rates. However, there are several limitations to this methodology.

- We collected data on all of USDA's food aid shipments and USAID's packaged food aid shipments. However, similar data on USAID's bulk food aid shipments were not available and our results cannot be generalized to those shipments. In order to address this limitation, we analyzed the award data, when feasible and appropriate, which include all shipments of food aid.
- We used a particular set of changes in the CPFA requirements to provide some insight into the effect of the CPFA requirements. However, these results cannot be generalized to other potential changes in the CPFA requirements. For example, our results cannot be generalized to show the effects of eliminating all CPFA requirements or of requiring all U.S. food aid to be shipped on U.S.-flag vessels.
- We controlled for a variety of factors that can affect the number of bids and the food aid shipping rates; however, it is still possible that some other factors we cannot control for drive the effect we observe. We conducted some sensitivity analysis to help address this limitation.

DATA SOURCES

We collected data on shipping awards and bids from USDA's Kansas City Commodity Office's (KCCO) Web Based Supply Chain Management System (WBSCM). The data covered USAID's packaged food aid and all of USDA's food aid shipments from April 2011 through fiscal year 2014.[71] KCCO implemented WBSCM in April 2011. USAID does not use WBSCM to procure shipping for its bulk food aid.[72]

The data on bids include information on all bids submitted by carriers to ship USAID's packaged food aid and all of USDA's food aid from April 2011 through fiscal year 2014. For each bid, the data include information on the carrier that submitted bids, the date of submission, the name of the vessel, the vessel type (bulker, liner, or tanker), the commodity, the implementing partner, the recipient country, the destination and discharge port, and the quantity of the order.

We conducted our analysis at the level of each solicitation line and constructed the data on bids to count the number of bids submitted for each solicitation line. Each agency announces solicitations for bids to ship food aid. Each solicitation includes a line for a specific amount of a specific commodity to be procured for a specific food aid program. For example, a recent solicitation for USAID included one line for 51,710 metric tons of sorghum for the World Food Program's food aid program in Sudan. We also included the information on the solicitation line such as the commodity, the implementing partner, the recipient country, the destination, and the quantity of the line. For the date of the solicitation, we used the date the first bid was submitted.[73]

The data on shipping awards includes two sets of data. One set is the bids that were actually awarded the shipping contract when KCCO applied the CPFA requirements. The second set is the bids that would have been awarded the shipping contract had the CPFA requirements not been applied. Both sets of data include information on the quantity of the solicitation line, the type of commodity, the agency (USAID or USDA), the implementing partner, the recipient country, the destination, the quantity allocated to each awarded bid, the type of vessel, and the total shipping cost. Each solicitation line may be split into more than one shipment. For example, half of a solicitation line may be shipped on U.S.-flag vessels and the other half on foreign-flag vessels. Again, we conducted our analysis at the level of each solicitation line and constructed both sets of data on shipping awards so that for each solicitation line, we calculated information such as the quantity allocated to U.S.- and foreign-flag vessels, the awarded cost of shipping on U.S.- and foreign-flag vessels, and the awarded shipping rate on U.S.- and foreign-flag vessels.

We merged the data on bids and the two sets of data on shipping awards for each solicitation line. When merging the two sets of data on shipping awards, only 75 (4 percent) of 1,712 solicitation lines did not match.

When merging the two sets of data on shipping awards with the data on bids, 676 (28 percent) of the 2,388 solicitation lines from the data on bids did not match the data on shipping awards. According to KCCO officials, the 676 solicitation lines that did not have a match with the data on shipping awards could be partly due to solicitation lines that were not awarded.[74] All solicitations lines from the data on shipping awards had a match in the data on bids.

For each set of data, we created a dummy variable which equals to 0 for any solicitation line before the CPFA requirements change and 1 for after.

ANALYSIS OF THE NUMBER OF OCEAN FREIGHT BIDS

Data source. For the analysis of the number of ocean freight bids carriers submitted, we used the data on bids, which included 2,388 solicitation lines.[75] Even though not all of these solicitation lines would eventually be awarded in the data on shipping awards, we focused on this larger data set because prior to the award process, the carriers cannot predict which solicitation lines would be awarded. Therefore, the number of bids is better captured by the full set of data on bids.

Summary statistics. Comparing the average number of bids before and after the changes, we found that the overall number of bids increased from around 7 to around 10 bids (see table 4). The average number of bids from U.S.-flag bids remained roughly unchanged and the average number of bids from foreign-flag vessels increased from around 2 to around 5.

We also compared the characteristics of the solicitations lines before and after the changes in the CPFA requirements to describe how USDA and USAID food aid programs may have changed. These included the composition of food aid by commodity type, the month of the solicitation line, the implementing partner, and the destination. We found few differences in the implementing partner and the type of commodity before and after the changes.

However, we did find differences in the destination and the month of the solicitation line. For example, the percentage of solicitation lines destined for Port-au-Prince, Haiti, decreased from 8 to 3 percent of solicitation lines after the changes in the CPFA requirements. The differences in these characteristics before and after the change emphasized the importance of controlling for these characteristics when comparing the number of bids before and after the changes. In our example of Port-Au- Prince, a solicitation line with food aid destined there was correlated with a higher number of bids. And since the percentage of solicitation lines destined there decreased after the change, the number of bids may have decreased due to this. However, if we observed a decrease only in bids, one may have erroneously attributed the decrease to the changes in the CPFA requirements if we did not control for the destination.

Table 4. Characteristics of Solicitation Lines before and after the Changes in the Cargo Preference for Food Aid Requirements, April 2011 through Fiscal Year 2014

Characteristic	Description	Average	Standard deviation	Average	Standard deviation	Difference
		Before change (937 solicitation lines)		After change (1,451 solicitation lines)		
Counts of bids for each solicitation line						
Number of bids	All bids, both winning and losing	6.63	3	9.65	5.46	3.02***
Number of bids from U.S.-flag vessels	All bids from U.S.- flag vessels	4.58	2.73	4.63	3.3	0.05
Number of bids from foreign-flag vessels	All bids from foreign- flag vessels	2.05	1.46	5.02	3.42	2.97***
Counts of vessels bidding for each solicitation line						
Number of vessels bidding[a]	Count of distinct vessel names bidding	4.72	1.73	5.95	2.51	1.22***
Number of U.S.-flag vessels bidding	Count of U.S.-flag vessel names	4.58	2.73	4.63	3.3	0.05
Number of foreign-flag vessels bidding	Count of foreign-flag vessel names	1.95	1.2	3.5	1.86	1.55***
Counts of carriers bidding for each solicitation line						
Number of carriers bidding	Count of distinct carrier names bidding	4.18	1.48	4.76	2.04	0.59***
Number of carriers submitting bids on U.S.-flag vessels	Count of carriers submitting bids on a U.S.-flag vessel	4.58	2.73	4.63	3.3	0.05
Number of carriers submitting bids on foreign-flag vessels	Count of carriers submitting bids on a foreign-flag vessel	1.73	1.17	2.89	1.71	1.16***
Commodity characteristics listed in solicitation line						
Tonnage	The weight of the food aid solicited	1207.89	2379.73	1099.49	2276.49	-108.4

Table 4. (Continued)

Characteristic	Description	Average	Standard deviation	Average	Standard deviation	Difference
		Before change (937 solicitation lines)		After change (1,451 solicitation lines)		
Proportion packaged food aid	Whether the solicitation line is for packaged (versus bulk) food aid	0.97	0.17	0.96	0.19	0
Type of commodity	A set of 21 dummy variables for each type of commodity in the solicitation line (e.g., corn is one type)	The difference before and after the changes was statistically significant for 6 of the 21 types of commodities.				
Month	A set of 12 dummy variables for the month in which the first bid was submitted for the solicitation line	The difference before and after the changes was statistically significant for 9 of the 12 months.				
Implementing partner[b]	A set of 36 dummy variables for the implementing partner (e.g., the World Food Program)	The difference before and after the changes was statistically significant for 10 of the 36 implementing partners.				
Destination	A set of 100 dummy variables for the destination of the food aid	The difference before and after the changes was statistically significant for 50 of the 100 destinations.				

Source: GAO analysis of U.S. Department of Agriculture (USDA) data. | GAO-15-666

Notes: Our analysis examined awards for all of USDA's solicitation lines and awards for USAID's packaged solicitation lines from April 2011 through fiscal year 2014. *** indicates statistical significance at the 99 percent level. ** indicates statistical significance at the 95 percent level. * indicates statistical significance at the 90 percent level. No stars indicates that the difference was not statistically significant.

[a] According to USAID officials, carriers may sometimes submit a bid with one or no vessel names but use another vessel to ship the food aid.

[b] Includes a dummy variable for food aid destined for USAID's prepositioning warehouses.

Table 5. Ordinary Least Square (OLS) Regression Results for the Total Number of Bids and the Number of Bids from U.S.-Flag and Foreign-Flag Vessels for Each Solicitation Line before and after the Changes in the Cargo Preference for Food Aid (CPFA) Requirements, April 2011 through Fiscal Year 2014

	Total number of bids	Number of bids from U.S.-flag vessels	Number of bids from foreign-flag vessels
Dummy for CPFA changes	**3.43*** **	0.34	3.09***
Standard error	**<0.42>**	<0.33>	<0.29>
Tonnage	**0.69*** **	0.26***	0.43***
Standard error	**<0.14>**	<0.05>	<0.11>
Inclusion of other independent variables			
Destination	**Yes**	Yes	Yes
Month	**Yes**	Yes	Yes
Recipient	**Yes**	Yes	Yes
Packaged food aid	**No**	No	No
Type of commodity	**No**	No	No
Adjusted R squared	**0.57**	0.43	0.59
Number of solicitation lines		**2,388**	

Source: GAO analysis of U.S. Department of Agriculture (USDA) data. | GAO-15-666

Note: To estimate the change in the number of bids after the changes in the CPFA requirements, we controlled for the factors that could affect the carriers' bidding behavior, including total tonnage in the solicitation and the month the first bid for the solicitation line was submitted. We created a dummy variable that equals 0 for any solicitation before the CPFA requirements change and 1 for after. The coefficient on the dummy variable indicates whether the number of bids changed after the changes. Our analysis examined awards for all of USDA's solicitation lines and awards for USAID's packaged solicitation lines from April 2011 through fiscal year 2014. We clustered our standard errors at the level of the solicitation. Controlling for destination added a set of 100 dummy variables and increased the adjusted R squared by 0.30 when the dependent variable was the total number of bids. *** indicates statistical significance at the 99 percent level. No stars indicate that the change in the shipping rate was not statistically significant.

Regression model and results. To compare the number of bids for each solicitation line before and after the changes in the CPFA requirements, we estimated ordinary least square (OLS) regressions using the following equation.

$$y_i = \alpha + \beta Change_i + \delta X_i + \varepsilon_i$$

We estimated this equation for solicitation line *i* where $Change_i$ is a dummy for before and after the CPFA changes, X_i is a set of solicitation line characteristics including the tonnage, implementing partner, destination of the food aid, and the month the first bid was submitted for the solicitation line, and ε_i is the error term. The dependent variable, y_i is the number of bids for each solicitation line *i*.

Using this model specification, we found that the total number of bids increased by 3.43 and the number of bids from foreign-flag vessels increased by 3.09 (see table 5). The increase in the number of bids from U.S.-flag vessels was not statistically significant.[76] We also found that the number of foreign-flag vessels and foreign-flag carriers bidding for each solicitation line increased by 1.58 vessels and 1.22 carriers. We found that the number of U.S.-flag vessels and carriers bidding decreased by 0.26 vessels and 0.60 carriers. This suggests that some of the increase in the number of foreign-flag bids may be from more carriers and vessels participating. The results from the OLS regressions are robust to the inclusion of different sets of control variables. We do not control for a dummy for whether the solicitation line was for bulk or packaged food aid and for the type of commodity because controlling for them did not significantly improve the explanatory power of the model.

Potential limitations and sensitivity analysis. The main limitation with our methodology is that we cannot control for all factors that may affect the number of bids from U.S.-flag and foreign-flag vessels. For example, the number of U.S.-flag vessels available to ship food aid declined during our study period from April 2011 through fiscal year 2014. However, we did not include data on the trends in the vessels in our analysis. So even though the changes of the CPFA requirements may have increased the number of bids from U.S.-flag vessels, the decline in the number of U.S.- flag vessels may have decreased the number of bids, thereby nullifying any increases from the changes in the CPFA requirements. Since the number of U.S.-flag vessels available for food aid was not included in our analysis, we may have erroneously found that the changes did not change the number of bids from U.S.-flag vessels.

- Figure 11 adds validity to our methodology in identifying the effect of the changes of the CPFA requirements on the number of bids from foreign-flag vessels. We estimated 39 OLS regressions, 1 for each month between May 2011 and July 2014, as the dummy variable so we could test for a break point. For each month, we created a dummy variable set to 0 for any solicitation line before that month and to 1 for any solicitation line after that month. We estimated 39 separate OLS regressions with each regression controlling for 1 month dummy variable in addition to the tonnage, implementing partner, and destination of the food aid, and the month the first bid was submitted for the solicitation line. Figure 11 shows the coefficient and the 99 percent confidence interval around the coefficient on the month dummy variable from each of the 39 OLS regressions. We found that the largest coefficient is for July 2012, the month of the changes in the CPFA requirements. These results show that the largest increase in the number of bids from foreign-flag vessels occurred in July 2012, the month of the CPFA changes. This suggests that the changes in the CPFA requirements had a larger effect on the number of bids from foreign-flag vessels than any other changes that may have happened between from April 2011 through fiscal year 2014.
- We estimated the OLS regression models using data from 6 months before and after the changes; we found even larger and statistically significant increases in the number of bids, especially from foreign-flag vessels. Finding the increase in the number of bids from foreign-flag vessels using data for this shorter period builds more confidence in the robustness of our results.[77]

Analysis of Food Aid Shipping Rates

Data source. To estimate the shipping rates of the winning bids before and after the changes in the CPFA requirements, we analyzed data on shipping awards, which included 1,712 solicitation lines.

Summary statistics. We found that the average overall shipping rates declined slightly from $258 per metric ton to $252 per metric ton after the changes (see table 6).[78] For U.S.-flag vessels, the average shipping rates increased from $290 to $309 per metric ton after the changes. The average shipping rates remained unchanged after the changes for foreign-flag vessels.[79]

We also compared the characteristics of the solicitations lines before and after the changes in the CPFA requirements. These characteristics included the composition of the food aid by the type of commodities, agency, the month of the solicitation line, the implementing partner, and the destination. We found few differences in the implementing partner and the type of commodity before and after the changes. However, we did find differences in the destination and the month of the solicitation line. These results are consistent with those from the data on bids since the data on awards is a subset of the data on bids and represents 72 percent of the solicitation lines in the data on bids.

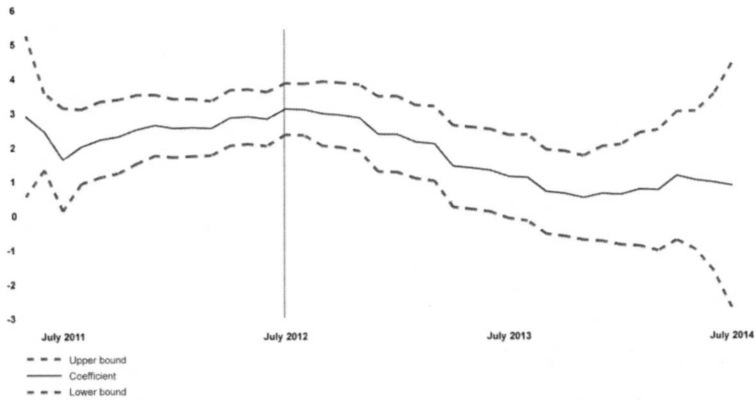

Source: GAO analysis of U.S. Department of Agriculture data. | GAO-15-666

Note: We estimated 39 OLS regressions, 1 with each month between May 2011 and July 2014 as a dummy variable. For each month, we created a dummy variable set to 0 for any solicitation line before that month and to 1 for any solicitation line after that month. We estimated 39 separate OLS regressions with each regression controlling for 1 month dummy variable in addition to the tonnage, implementing partner, and destination of the food aid, and the month the first bid was submitted for the solicitation line. The coefficient on the month dummy variable indicates whether the number of bids changed after that month. The upper and lower bounds delineate the 99 percent confidence interval. Our analysis examined awards for all of the Department of Agriculture's solicitation lines and awards for the United States Agency for International Development's packaged solicitation lines from April 2011 through fiscal year 2014. We clustered our standard errors at the level of the solicitation.

Figure 11. Coefficients on Dummy Variables before and after Each Month from May 2011 through July 2014 from 39 Ordinary Least Square (OLS) Regressions of Number of Bids from Foreign-Flag Vessels on Control Variables.

Table 6. Characteristics of Solicitation Lines before and after the Changes in the Cargo Preference for Food Aid Requirements, April 2011 through Fiscal Year 2014

Characteristic	Description	Average	Standard deviation	Average	Standard deviation	Difference
		Before changes (644 solicitation lines)		After changes (1,068 solicitation lines)		
Shipping rates (per metric ton) of winning bid						
Shipping rates[a]	The total shipping cost divided by the tonnage awarded	258.44	118.25	251.48	140.57	-6.96
Shipping rates on U.S.-flag vessels	The shipping cost of U.S.-flag vessels divided by the tonnage awarded to U.S.-flag vessels	289.81	131.92	308.52	163.19	18.72**
Shipping rates from foreign-flag vessels	The shipping cost of foreign-flag vessels divided by the tonnage awarded to foreign-flag vessels	201.04	63	201.79	103.34	0.75
Agency for solicitation line						
USAID[b]	A dummy variable for whether the solicitation line is for USAID (versus USDA)	0.72	0.45	0.74	0.44	0.02
Commodity characteristics in solicitation line						
Tonnage	The weight of the food aid solicited	1358.21	2466.95	1239.19	2380.17	-119.03
Packaged food aid	A dummy variable for whether the solicitation line is for packaged (versus bulk) food aid	0.97	0.18	0.96	0.2	-0.01
Type of commodity[c]	A set of 20 dummy variables for each type of commodity in the solicitation line (e.g., corn is one type)	The difference before and after the changes was statistically significant for 3of the 20 types of commodities.				
Month	A set of 12 dummy variables for the month in which the first bid was	The difference before and after the changes was statistically significant for 9 of the 12 months.				

Table 6. (Continued)

Characteristic	Description	Before changes (644 solicitation lines) Average	Before changes (644 solicitation lines) Standard deviation	After changes (1,068 solicitation lines) Average	After changes (1,068 solicitation lines) Standard deviation	Difference
	submitted for the solicitation line					
Implementing partner[d]	A set of 36 dummy variables for the implementing partner (e.g., the World Food Program)	The difference before and after the changes was statistically significant for 11 of the 36 implementing partners.				
Destination[c]	A set of 97 dummy variables for the destination of the food aid	The difference before and after the changes was statistically significant for 43 of the 97 destinations.				

Source: GAO analysis of U.S. Department of Agriculture (USDA) data. | GAO-15-666

Notes: Our analysis examined awards for all of USDA's solicitation lines and awards for USAID's packaged solicitation lines from April 2011 through fiscal year 2014. *** indicates statistical significance at the 99 percent level. ** indicates statistical significance at the 95 percent level. * indicates statistical significance at the 90 percent level. No stars indicates that the difference was not statistically significant.

[a] For the shipping rate of packaged food aid, we used the gross shipping rate, which includes the cost of shipping the bags containing the food aid. According to USAID, USAID pays the carriers based on the gross shipping rate.

[b] The data on shipping awards identify which solicitations are for USAID and USDA, but the data on bids do not.

[c] Since the data on shipping awards have fewer solicitation lines than the data on bids, some destinations and types of commodities in the data on bids are not included in the data on shipping awards.

[d] Includes a dummy variable for food aid destined for USAID's prepositioning warehouses.

Regression model and results. To compare the shipping rates for each solicitation line before and after the changes in the CPFA requirements, we estimated OLS regressions using the following equation.

$$y_i = \alpha + \beta\ Change_i + \delta X_i + \varepsilon_i$$

We estimated this equation for solicitation line *i* where $Change_i$ is a dummy for before and after the CPFA changes; X_i is a set of solicitation line characteristics including the tonnage, implementing partner, and destination of the food aid, and the month the first bid was submitted for the solicitation line;

and ε_i is the error term. y_i is the natural logarithm of the shipping rate for each solicitation line *i*.[80]

Table 7. Ordinary Least Square (OLS) Regression Results for the Natural Logarithm of Shipping Rates before and after the Changes in the Cargo Preference for Food Aid (CPFA) Requirements, April 2011 through Fiscal Year 2014

	Log of overall shipping rates	**Log of shipping rates on U.S.-flag vessels**	**Log of shipping rates on foreign-flag vessels**
Dummy for CPFA changes	-0.065*	0.039	-0.086***
Standard error	<0.036>	<0.027>	<0.019>
Tonnage	0.003	-0.037***	-0.022***
Standard error	<0.007>	<0.010>	<0.008>
Inclusion of other independent variables			
Destination	Yes	Yes	Yes
Month	Yes	Yes	Yes
Recipient	Yes	Yes	Yes
Packaged food aid	No	No	No
Type of commodity	No	No	No
Adjusted R squared	0.643	0.811	0.801
Number of solicitation lines	1,712	1,037	809

Source: GAO analysis of U.S. Department of Agriculture (USDA) data. | GAO-15-666

Note: To estimate the change in the shipping rate after the changes in the CPFA requirements, we controlled for the factors that could affect the shipping rate, including total tonnage in the solicitation and the month the first bid for the solicitation line was submitted. The dependent variable is the natural logarithm of the shipping rate. We created a dummy variable that equals 0 for any solicitation before the CPFA requirements change and 1 for after. The coefficient on the dummy variable indicates whether the number of bids changed after the changes. Our analysis examined awards for all of USDA's solicitation lines and awards for USAID's packaged solicitation lines from April 2011 through fiscal year 2014. We clustered our standard errors at the level of the solicitation. Controlling for destination added a set of 97 dummy variables and increased the adjusted R squared by 0.544. *** indicates statistical significance at the 99 percent level. ** indicates statistical significance at the 95 percent level. * indicates statistical significance at the 90 percent level. No stars indicates that the change in the shipping rate was not statistically significant.

Table 8. Ordinary Least Square (OLS) Regression Results for the Natural Logarithm of Shipping Rates for the United States Agency for International Development (USAID) and the Department of Agriculture (USDA) before and after the Changes in the Cargo Preference for Food Aid (CPFA) Requirements, April 2011 through Fiscal Year 2014

	USAID			USDA		
	Log of overall shipping rates	**Log of shipping rates on U.S.-flag vessels**	**Log of shipping rates on foreign-flag vessels**	**Log of overall shipping rates**	**Log of shipping rates on U.S.-flag vessels**	**Log of shipping rates on foreign-flag vessels**
Dummy for CPFA change	-0.095***	0.047**	-0.095***	-0.021	-0.03	-0.071*
Standard error	<0.035>	<0.018>	<0.022>	<0.074>	<0.086>	<0.037>
Tonnage	0.009	-0.019***	-0.018**	-0.004	-0.059**	-0.039**
Standard error	<0.007>	<0.006>	<0.009>	<0.022>	<0.026>	<0.016>
Destination	Yes	Yes	Yes	Yes	Yes	Yes
Inclusion of other independent variables						
Month	Yes	Yes	Yes	Yes	Yes	Yes
Recipient	Yes	Yes	Yes	Yes	Yes	Yes
Packaged food aid	No	No	No	No	No	No
Type of commodity	No	No	No	No	No	No
Adjusted R squared	0.54	0.803	0.765	0.741	0.815	0.905
Number of solicitation lines	1,253	696	621	459	341	188

Source: GAO analysis of U.S. Department of Agriculture (USDA) data. | GAO-15-666

Note: To estimate the change in the shipping rate after the changes in the CPFA requirements, we controlled for the factors that could affect the shipping rate, including total tonnage in the solicitation and the month the first bid for the solicitation line was submitted. The dependent variable is the natural logarithm of the shipping rate. We created a dummy variable that equals 0 for any solicitation before the CPFA requirements change and 1 for after. The coefficient on the dummy variable indicates whether the number of bids changed after the changes. Our analysis examined awards for all of USDA's solicitation lines and awards for USAID's packaged solicitation lines from April 2011 through fiscal year 2014. We clustered our standard errors at the level of the solicitation. *** indicates statistical significance at the 99 percent level. ** indicates statistical significance at the 95 percent level. * indicates statistical significance at the 90 percent level. No stars indicates that the change in the shipping rate was not statistically significant.

Using this model, we found that the overall shipping rate decreased by around 6 percent (see table 7).[81] We also found that the shipping rates on foreign-flag vessels decreased by around 8 percent. The shipping rates on U.S.-flag vessels did not change. The results from the OLS regressions are robust to the inclusion of different sets of control variables. The estimates range from a decrease of around 6 percent to a decrease of around 8 percent. We do not control for a dummy for whether the solicitation line was for bulk or packaged food aid and for the type of commodity because controlling for them do not increase the adjusted R squared by much.

Compared with USDA, USAID is more flexible in applying the CPFA requirements. The percentage of food aid shipped on U.S.-flag vessels declined much more for USAID than for USDA after the changes in the CPFA requirements. Consistent with this difference between agencies, the shipping rates for USAID decreased, while those for USDA did not (see table 8).[82] The overall shipping rate decreased by around 9 percent for USAID, likely because of the increased use of foreign-flag vessels after the change and the 9 percent decrease in the shipping rates on those foreign-flag vessels.[83] The shipping rate on U.S.-flag vessels increased by around 5 percent for USAID.[84] For USDA, the overall shipping rate and the shipping rate on U.S.-flag vessels were unchanged, while the shipping rate on foreign-flag vessels decreased by around 7 percent.

Potential limitations and sensitivity analysis. The main limitation with our methodology is that we cannot control for all factors that may affect shipping rates. For example, the overall commercial shipping rates could have declined during the period of our data from April 2011 through fiscal year 2014. Some of the decrease in shipping rates could have been due to other factors that cause the overall decline instead of the changes in the CPFA requirements. While we did not obtain data on commercial shipping rates, we found two results that may ameliorate this limitation.

- Figure 12 adds validity to our methodology in identifying the effect of the changes of the CPFA requirements on USAID's shipping rates. We estimated 39 OLS regressions, 1 with each month between May 2011 and July 2014 as a dummy variable. For each month, we created a dummy variable set to 0 for any solicitation line before that month and to 1 for any solicitation line after that month. We estimated 39 separate OLS regressions with each regression controlling for 1 month dummy variable in addition to the tonnage, implementing partner, and destination of the food aid, and the month the first bid was submitted for the solicitation line. Figure 12 shows the coefficient and the 99 percent confidence interval around the coefficient on the month dummy variable from each of the 39 OLS regressions. We found that the smallest coefficients are for July and August 2012. These results show that the largest decline in USAID's shipping rates occurred in July 2012, the month of the CPFA changes. This suggests that the changes in the CPFA requirements had the larger effect on USAID's shipping rates than any other changes that may have happened between from April 2011 through fiscal year 2014.

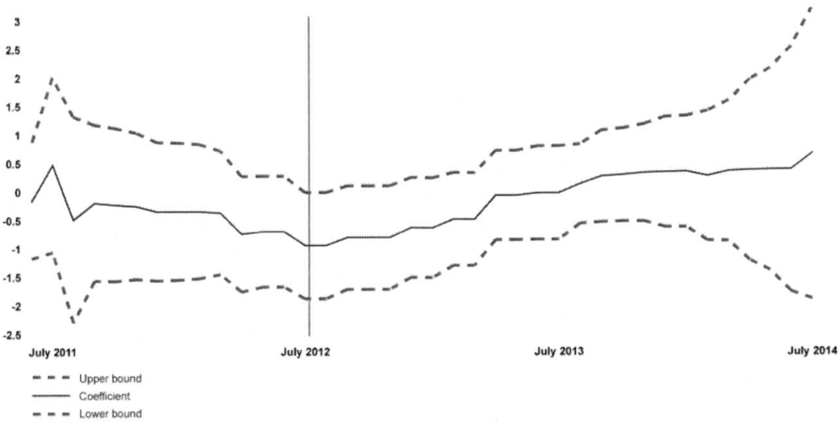

Source: GAO analysis of U.S. Department of Agriculture data. | GAO-15-66

Note: We estimated 39 OLS regressions, 1 for each month between May 2011 and July 2014. For each month, we created a dummy variable set to 0 for any solicitation line before that month and to 1 for any solicitation line after that month. We estimated 39 separate OLS regressions with each regression controlling for 1 month dummy variable in addition to the tonnage, implementing partner, and destination of the food aid, and the month the first bid was submitted for the solicitation line. The coefficient on the month dummy variable indicates whether the shipping rate changed after that month. The upper and lower bounds delineate the 99 percent confidence interval. Our analysis examined awards for USAID's packaged solicitation lines from April 2011 through fiscal year 2014. We clustered our standard errors at the level of the solicitation.

Figure 12. Coefficients on Dummy Variables before and after Each Month from May 2011 through July 2014 from Ordinary Least Square (OLS) Regressions of the Natural Logarithm of the United States Agency for International Development's (USAID) Overall Shipping Rate on Controls Variables.

- When we estimated the OLS regression models only for the period 6 months before and after the changes, we found even larger and statistically significant decreases in the shipping rates on foreign-flag vessels. For this shorter period, there was likely to have been less change in other factors such as overall commercial shipping rates. For USDA, the decrease in the overall shipping rate became larger and statistically significant, likely because of the large decrease in the shipping rates on foreign-flag vessels. However, for USAID, the decrease in the overall shipping rate was not statistically significant, likely because of the larger standard errors. Finding the decrease in the shipping rates on foreign-flag vessels for this shorter period builds some more confidence in the robustness of the result.[85]

APPENDIX III: THE MARITIME ADMINISTRATION'S FAIR AND REASONABLE DETERMINATIONS

The Cargo Preference Act of 1954 requires civilian federal government agencies to ship on U.S.-flag vessels only to the extent that such vessels are available at "fair and reasonable rates." The fair and reasonable provision helps ensure that U.S.-flag vessels do not overcharge federal agencies required to ship on U.S.-flag vessels. The Maritime Administration (MARAD) will find a rate to be fair and reasonable if it is less than or equal to MARAD's estimate of the cost of the voyage in question plus a reasonable profit. MARAD calculates fair and reasonable rates for ships chartered to carry shiploads of bulk and packaged agricultural commodities. Rates are also determined for bulk agricultural commodities carried by liner-service vessels. For other cargoes carried on liner-service vessels, conference rates are paid, which MARAD maintains are inherently fair and reasonable.

MARAD makes a separate cost estimate for each voyage that it is asked to investigate. It bases its estimate on operating cost information supplied annually by the ship owner and certified by a corporate officer and on information specific to the voyage in question. Additionally, MARAD factors the return trip into the cost of the voyage. MARAD assumes that the vessel will return empty of cargo. If the vessel does carry cargo on the return trip, it must report this to the shipper agency, and if requested by the shipper agency MARAD will make an adjustment to the fair and reasonable rate. MARAD also allows for a reasonable profit on a 5-year running average derived from transportation companies in the Fortune 500 as well as the U.S. corporate sector in general. Currently, this profit factor is about 19 percent.

MARAD requests ship owners to supply the following cost information each year:

- normal operating speed;
- daily fuel consumption at normal operating speed;
- daily fuel consumption while in port;
- type of fuel used;
- total capitalized vessel costs, for example, cost of vessel acquisition;
- vessel operating cost information for the prior calendar year; and
- number of vessel operating days for the vessels for the prior calendar year (this information is used to determine daily operating cost).

Additionally, MARAD collects the following information for each voyage for which a fair and reasonable rate is calculated:

- port expenses for ports the vessel is scheduled to visit—for example, fees for pilots and custom charges;
- cargo expenses—for example, fees for stevedores and off-loading equipment, and
- canal expenses—for example, fees for tolls.

APPENDIX IV: COMPLETE LIST OF STAKEHOLDER OPTIONS AND COUNTS

Table 9 lists 27 options to improve the sustainability of the oceangoing U.S.-flag fleet, including food aid–carrying U.S.-flag vessels, derived from semistructured interviews with a nongeneralizable sample of 29 stakeholders knowledgeable about cargo preference for food aid (CPFA) issues.[86] For each option, we list the number out of 18 stakeholders who selected the option as one of their top three options. For each option, we also list the number out of 7 maritime industry stakeholders who selected the option as one of their top three options and the number out of 11 other maritime stakeholders who selected the option as one of their top three options. For a detailed description of our scope and methodology for these semistructured interviews, see appendix I.

Table 9. Numbers of Stakeholders, Maritime Industry Stakeholders, and Other Maritime Stakeholders Who Selected Options as Being among Their Top Three Choices

Options	Overall stakeholders (18 total responses)	Maritime industry stakeholders (7 total responses)	Other maritime stakeholders (11 responses)
Increase cargo preference for food aid (CPFA) minimum requirement from 50 to 75 percent	3	1	2
Increase CPFA minimum requirement from 50 to 100 percent	3	2	1
Modify the 3-year waiting period imposed on foreign vessels that acquire U.S.-flag registry before they are eligible for carriage of preference food aid cargo	1	0	1
Eliminate the 3-year waiting period imposed on foreign vessels that acquire U.S.-flag registry before they are eligible for carriage of preference food aid cargo	4	1	3
Reinstate Ocean Freight Differential and Twenty Percent Excess Freight reimbursements	3	1	2
Eliminate CPFA and create a Department of Defense program to provide military sealift capability	3	0	3
Increase all cargo preference to 100 percent	4	3	1
Determine the minimum number of vessels and mariners needed to sustain the U.S.-flag fleet	2	0	2
Subsidize U.S.-flag fleet vessels	3	1	2
Give priority berthing rights to U.S.-flag fleet vessels	0	0	0
Reform tax law that may negatively affect the U.S.-flag fleet	3	0	3
Reform tort law that may negatively affect the U.S.-flag fleet	3	1	2
Reform U.S. shipping standards to better align with international standards	0	0	0
Eliminate mariner nationality requirements for U.S.-flag fleet vessels	0	0	0
Harmonize customs duties, especially for North American Free Trade Agreement countries, and bill of lading so shipped cargo is treated the same as cargo moving on land	0	0	0

Table 9. (Continued)

Options	Overall stakeholders (18 total responses)	Maritime industry stakeholders (7 total responses)	Other maritime stakeholders (11 responses)
Increase U.S. shipbuilding	1	0	1
Develop a single government-wide policy to implement CPFA	1	1	0
Educate U.S. government agencies that the CPFA minimum requirement of 50 percent is the minimum and not the maximum	1	0	1
Do not require agricultural cargo preference compliance by country	2	0	2
Increase the Maritime Administration's monitoring and enforcement of its statutory authority	4	3	1
Enforce cargo preference requirements for all U.S. government agencies	2	2	0
Improve commercial terms in cargo preference contracts between U.S. government agencies and U.S. carriers	1	1	0
Improve the food aid procurement/ supply chain process to include (market) efficiencies	3	0	3
Increase cooperation between the United States Agency for International Development and the United States Department of Agriculture	0	0	0
Increase funding for U.S. food aid programs	4	3	1
Provide multi-year funding for U.S. food aid programs	2	1	1
Increase the percentage of food aid shipped on bulk vessels	1	0	1
Total number of selections:	**54**	**21**	**33**

Source: GAO analysis of stakeholder selections. | GAO-15-666

For a summary of the key results from our semistructured interview and follow-up effort, see figure 10 in this report. In addition to these earlier observations, it is important to note that our analysis of stakeholder selection of options to improve the sustainability of the oceangoing U.S.- flag fleet, including food aid–carrying U.S.-flag vessels, reveals instances of overlap to some degree among options selected by maritime industry stakeholders and other maritime stakeholders. Specifically, 10 of the 27 options were selected by 1 or more stakeholder from each of the two categories. These 10 options were (1) increase CPFA minimum requirement from 50 to 75 percent, (2) increase CPFA minimum requirement from 50 to 100 percent, (3) eliminate the 3-year waiting period imposed on foreign vessels that acquire U.S.-flag registry before they are eligible for carriage of preference food aid cargo, (4) reinstate Ocean Freight Differential and Twenty Percent Excess Freight reimbursements, (5) increase all cargo preference to 100 percent, (6) subsidize U.S.-flag fleet vessels, (7) reform tort law that may negatively affect the U.S.-flag fleet, (8) increase the Maritime Administration's monitoring and enforcement of its statutory authority, (9) increase funding for U.S. food aid programs, and (10) provide multiyear funding for U.S. food aid programs. However, no options were selected by 2 or more stakeholders from each of the two categories. Finally, 5 of the 27 options were not selected by any stakeholders from either category as part of their top 3 options. These 5 options were (1) give priority berthing rights to U.S.-flag fleet vessels; (2) reform U.S. shipping standards to better align with international standards; (3) eliminate mariner nationality requirements for U.S.-flag fleet vessels; (4) harmonize customs duties, especially for NAFTA countries, and bill of lading so shipped cargo is treated the same as cargo moving on land; and (5) increase cooperation between the U.S. Agency for International Development (USAID) and the U.S. Department of Agriculture (USDA).

End Notes

[1] Through our discussions with knowledgeable agency officials and stakeholders, we found that there is no agency designation or agreed-upon term for cargo preference for food aid. Although it has sometimes been referred to as "agricultural cargo preference" in academic literature, we found that this phrase was confusing to some practitioners.

[2] Sealift is the process of transporting DOD and other federal agency equipment and supplies required during peacetime and war. We are only analyzing cargo preference for food aid and not for other government cargo. Our report will not examine the extent to which cargo preference for food aid addresses the intended objective of cargo preference on maintaining the financial viability of U.S.-flag vessel operating companies. According to MARAD, it does not have current and readily available data on oceanborne commerce carried by U.S.-flag vessels, but a past MARAD study showed that U.S.-flag vessels carried a declining portion of oceanborne commerce from 1946 to 2002.

[3] Our report will examine only the oceangoing portion of the U.S.-flag fleet that would include vessels that transport food aid internationally. Our report does not focus on vessels that are subject to the Jones Act, a U.S. law that applies to cargo shipped by waterborne transportation between two U.S. points.

[4] Our report focuses on the ocean transportation of commodities procured and shipped for three U.S. international food aid programs: Title II Food for Peace, Food for Progress, and McGovern-Dole International Food for Education and Child Nutrition.

[5] Bulk commodities, such as free-flowing grain and vegetable oil, are those directly loaded and shipped in an ocean vessels' cargo hold. Packaged commodities are those shipped in woven polypropylene bags, multiwalled paper bags, plastic containers, or steel cans and drums. We

obtained bid data to ship all USDA food aid and USAID's packaged food aid. We did not include bid data to ship USAID's bulk food aid because these data were not available in the database provided, which was implemented in April 2011. USAID's data of awarded bids (award data) show that bulk commodities accounted for about 50 percent of USAID total commodities in the past few years. However, we did include USAID's bulk commodities in our analysis of all USAID's and USDA's award data.

[6] During our semi-structured interviews we verbally explained to stakeholders that our review is only focused on the oceangoing vessels of the U.S.-flag fleet and our review is on the topic of cargo preference for food aid.

[7] For the purposes of this report, we use the term "implementing partners" as entities such as NGOs that are awarded U.S. government grants to carry out food assistance activities overseas, and international humanitarian aid organizations. NGOs include international humanitarian aid organizations; international and local private voluntary organizations; and other entities.

[8] We further categorized stakeholders that self-identified as freight forwarders as exclusive freight forwarders or implementing partner freight forwarders. For the purposes of this report, an "exclusive freight forwarder" refers to an agent that provides services for a shipper—in this case, either the U.S. government or an implementing partner. Such services include advising on freight costs, among other costs, and preparing and filing the bill of lading and other required documentation. We categorized "exclusive freight forwarder" under "maritime industry stakeholders." An "implementing partner freight forwarder" refers to a shipper that is working in partnership with an "exclusive freight forwarder," which we categorized under "other maritime stakeholders."

[9] We followed up with all 29 stakeholders, but 2 (both other maritime stakeholders) did not prefer any of the suggested options and 9 (6 maritime industry stakeholders and 3 other maritime stakeholders) declined to comment further or did not provide a response after contacting them multiple times. For example, 2 of these 9 stakeholders declined to comment further because their organizations' leadership advised them not to do so.

[10] Intermodal capacity includes dry cargo ships, equipment, terminal facilities and intermodal management services.

[11] Established by the Maritime Security Act of 1996 (Pub. L. No. 104-239) and reauthorized in the Maritime Security Act (MSA) of 2003 (Pub. L. No. 108-136, div. C, Title XXXV) and the National Defense Authorization Act (NDAA) of 2013 (Pub. L. No. 112-239, § 3508), MSP requires that the Secretary of Transportation, in consultation with the Secretary of Defense, establish a fleet of active, commercially viable, militarily useful, privately owned vessels to meet national defense and other security requirements. The NDAA of 2013 extended the program until 2025 and authorized $186 million for fiscal years 2016, 2017, and 2018; $210 million for fiscal years 2019, 2020, and 2021; and $222 million for fiscal years 2022, 2023, 2024, and 2025 to support the operation of 60 U.S.-flag vessels in the foreign commerce of the United States. Participating operators are required to make their ships and commercial transportation resources available, through VISA and Voluntary Tanker Agreement programs, upon request by the Secretary of Defense during times of war or national emergency or whenever the Secretary of Defense determines that it is necessary for national security or contingency operation. Tanker vessels enrolled in MSP are required to be in the Voluntary Tanker Agreement, another program similar to VISA that provides DOD with access to tanker vessels to provide commercial sealift and intermodal capacity. According to DOD and MARAD officials, only a few tanker vessels transport food aid.

[12] According to DOD officials, the guidance pertaining to military usefulness was rescinded in February 2012; interim guidance was issued in October 2013 to be used by the planning community, but it did not define military usefulness. DOD officials noted that a definition for the term "militarily useful" would be included in the Logistics Supplement to the *Joint Strategic Capabilities Plan,* expected to be published by September 2015. In the meantime,

the rescinded document is used as temporary guidance to determine a vessel's military usefulness.

[13] According to DOD officials, militarily useful sealift is defined in terms of dry cargo and liquid cargo. Dry cargo ships have the ability to carry a minimum of 2,000 long tons of cargo and the ability to carry, without significant modification, unit equipment, ammunition, or sustaining supplies. Liquid cargo ships have a capacity within the range of 2,000 to 100,000 deadweight ton, and a sustained speed in excess of 12 knots.

[14] In addition, MARAD has 2 special mission vessels for missile defense purposes.

[15] Vessels in the reserve sealift fleet have maintenance crews of about 6 to15 commercial merchant mariners that are supplemented by additional mariners during activations.

[16] The STCW Convention and STCW code set forth standards for training and certification for merchant mariners. The International Maritime Organization amended the STCW convention and STCW Code on June 25, 2010. These amendments entered into force for all ratifying countries on Jan. 1, 2012. USCG published a final rule on Dec. 24, 2013, that implements the STCW, including the 2010 amendments. 78 Fed. Reg. 77,796. Amended regulations include all STCW requirements for training, assessment and service. Among other things, mariners must meet the additional training requirements specified in the regulations for specific endorsements sought by Dec. 31, 2016. Full compliance with the requirements must be met by Jan. 1, 2017. MARAD officials expressed concern that these new requirements will cause the number of U.S. mariners with STCW and unlimited tonnage endorsements to decline significantly.

[17] GAO, *U.S. Merchant Marine: Maritime Administration Should Assess Potential Mariner-Training Needs.* GAO-14-212 (Washington, D.C.: Jan. 31, 2014).

[18] The World Food Program defines emergencies as "urgent situations in which there is clear evidence that an event or series of events has occurred which causes human suffering or imminently threatens human lives or livelihoods and which the government concerned has not the means to remedy; and it is a demonstrably abnormal event or series of events which produces dislocation in the life of a community on an exceptional scale." In nonemergency situations, U.S. commodities may be provided to address chronic hunger.

[19] USDA officials also use the term "sales order" for "commodity request."

[20] For more information on the Web Based Supply Chain Management System, see GAO, *International Food Aid: Better Agency Collaboration Needed to Assess and Improve Emergency Food Aid Procurement System*, GAO-14-22 (Washington, D.C.: Mar. 26, 2014).

[21] USAID may use other delivery methods such as overseas prepositioning, domestic prepositioning, and diversion. For more information see GAO, *International Food Aid: Prepositioning Speeds Delivery of Emergency Aid, but Additional Monitoring of Time Frames and Costs Is Needed*, GAO-14-277 (Washington, D.C.: Mar. 5, 2014).

[22] Department of Transportation, Maritime Administration, *Comparison of U.S. and Foreign Flag Operating Costs* (September 2011).

[23] USDA developed WBSCM, with USAID's input, to manage domestic and international food aid procurement. WBSCM was implemented and began collecting data in April 2011.

[24] To compare the cost of shipping food aid with and without the CPFA requirements, we analyzed the bids submitted in response to USDA and USAID's solicitations for ocean freight to ship all of USDA's food aid and USAID's packaged food aid from April 2011 through fiscal year 2014. For each solicitation, we compared the bids that were awarded to ship food aid and the bids that would have been awarded a contract had the CPFA requirements not been applied, which is a conservative way to measure the cost of CPFA requirements. However, this estimate may be lower than the full cost of the CPFA requirements because it is based on actual bids that would have been awarded a contract had the CPFA requirements not been applied, rather than bids that would have been awarded a contract if the CPFA requirements did not exist. If CPFA requirements did not exist, there might be more bids and lower shipping cost. For example, we found that the number of

foreign-flag bids increased after relaxing the CPFA requirements, which led to lower shipping rates.

[25] USAID used a different methodology to estimate the cost of shipping food aid with the CFPA requirements. USAID compared the cost of shipping food aid on U.S.-flag liner vessels with commercial liner shipping rates. USAID did not provide an estimate using its methodology for liner vessels from April 2011 through July 6, 2012. Therefore, we calculated the cost of shipping with the CFPA requirements using USAID's methodology and found that from April 2011 through July 6, 2012, the cost was 27 percent higher than if the food aid had been shipped on foreign-flag liner vessels. In contrast, for similar shipments and a similar period, we found that the cost of shipping with the CFPA requirements was 12 percent higher than if the requirements had not been applied when we used the methodology of this report.

[26] Pub. L. No. 99-198, § 1142. As previously described in figure 1, the ocean freight differential requirement was repealed in July 2012, while the excess freight provision was repealed in December 2013.

[27] 46 U.S.C. § 55305(b).

[28] This court order was a product of an agreement by litigating parties to settle the lawsuit.

[29] We controlled for factors that could affect the shipping rates, including the implementing partner, the destination, and the month the winning bid for the solicitation was submitted. We created a dummy variable which equals 0 for any solicitation before the changes in the CPFA requirements and 1 for after. The coefficient on the dummy variable indicates whether the shipping rate for that solicitation changed after the changes in the requirements. Our analysis examined awards for all of USDA's solicitations and awards for USAID's packaged solicitations from April 2011 through fiscal year 2014. See app. II for a detailed discussion of the model structure, a full list of independent variables, and our complete results.

[30] GAO, *Foreign Assistance: Various Challenges Impede the Efficiency and Effectiveness of U.S. Food Aid*, GAO-07-560 (Washington, D.C.: April 13, 2007), and *International Food Assistance: Local and Regional Procurement Can Enhance the Efficiency of U.S. Food Aid, but Challenges May Constrain Its Implementation,* GAO-09-570 (Washington, D.C.: May 29, 2009).

[31] As of March 2015, the number had further declined to 167 U.S.-flag vessels. These numbers represent self-propelled commercially operated vessels and integrated tug barge units employed internationally and in the coastwise trades. The number of vessels in the oceangoing U.S.-flag fleet peaked in 1951 and has since declined. Our analysis, however, focuses on changes occurring since 2005.

[32] U.S. Department of Transportation, Maritime Administration, *A Report to Congress: Impacts of Reductions in Government Impelled Cargo on the U.S, Merchant Marine* (April, 21 2015).

[33] The decline in food aid commodities provided by the U.S. government has been driven by many factors, including increases in (1) commodity and shipping costs, (2) food aid assistance in the form of cash or vouchers and local and regional procurement, and (3) the use of specialized—and therefore costly— products to meet the nutritional needs of the most vulnerable groups.

[34] MARAD officials noted that although all of the commercially-owned vessels in the oceangoing U.S.-flag fleet are eligible to transport food aid cargo, some vessels, such as roll-on, roll-off vessels, typically do not participate in the food aid trade.

[35] MARAD's database does not include positions available in tug and barge combinations, many of which carried food aid in 2005.

[36] *A Report to Congress: Impacts of Reductions in Government Impelled Cargo on the U.S. Merchant Marine.*

[37] Includes 86 oceangoing Jones Act–eligible vessels as well as 81 participating in international trade. These vessels are oceangoing, self-propelled, cargo-carrying U.S.-flag vessels of 1,000 gross tons and above in foreign and domestic trades.

[38] DOD utilizes a seven-level priority system when selecting among the vessels that provide capacity to support DOD needs. However DOD officials told us that VISA participants are not granted exclusivity, particularly if their rates are too high. The priority system is as follows: (1) U.S.-flag vessel capacity operated by a VISA participant and U.S.-flag vessel sharing agreement (VSA) capacity of a VISA participant, (2) U.S.-flag vessel capacity operated by a VISA nonparticipant, (3) combination of U.S.-flag/foreign-flag vessel capacity operated by a VISA participant and combination U.S.-flag/foreign-flag VSA capacity of a VISA participant, (4) combination U.S.-flag/foreign-flag vessel capacity operated by a VISA nonparticipant, (5) U.S.-owned or -operated foreign-flag vessel capacity and VSA capacity of a VISA participant, (6) U.S.-owned or -operated foreign-flag vessel capacity and VSA capacity of a VISA nonparticipant, (7) foreign-owned or -operated foreign-flag vessel capacity of a VISA nonparticipant.

[39] According to the United States Transportation Command, vessels enrolled in MSP are required to also be enrolled in VISA or the Voluntary Tanker Agreement. VISA and Voluntary Tanker Agreement are the only programs DOD would activate during times of war. However, since MSP participants are required to be enrolled in VISA or the Voluntary Tanker Agreement, it is probable that many of those activated would be vessels also in MSP.

[40] In addition, MARAD has 2 special mission vessels for missile defense purposes.

[41] National Security Directive 28 directs DOD to determine the requirements for sealift, among other things, and DOT to determine whether adequate manpower is available to meet such requirements. According to DOD officials, DOD has determined the number of vessels—both commercial and those in the reserve sealift fleet—that would be required to meet its needs under different contingency scenarios and communicated that to MARAD.

[42] According to MARAD officials, there are 207 vessels that utilize the same type of mariners needed to crew the surge sealift vessels, which they expect will continue to operate during the same period during which the reserve surge fleet is activated. MARAD officials explained that these vessels comprise those in the U.S.-flag fleet that have a gross tonnage of at least 1,600, in addition to passenger vessels of the appropriate tonnage and privately owned fleet support vessels on charter to the Military Sealift Command that are not counted in MARAD's list of 167 oceangoing U.S. flag vessels because of their specialized usages.

[43] During the course of our review, MARAD provided the estimated number of mariners required for prolonged full activation as 12,658 based on 211 vessels. In commenting on our draft report, however, DOT provided another estimate of 13,034 based on 207 vessels. While MARAD officials outlined some factors and high-level calculations they utilize when computing such an estimate, we could not assess the reliability or accuracy of either estimate because MARAD did not have a final report that documented and presented precise calculations and methods that they used. In addition, MARAD did not explain why the number of mariners required had risen even though the number of vessels had been reduced. We therefore were unable to verify the details of their estimates.

[44] *A Report to Congress: Impacts of Reductions in Government Impelled Cargo on the U.S. Merchant Marine.*

[45] USCG maintains mariner credential data in the USCG Merchant Mariner Licensing and Documentation System. We obtained data available since 2008. The number of mariners represents those for master, chief mate, and officer in charge of a navigational watch with STCW and unlimited tonnage endorsement and the number of engineers with STCW and unlimited horsepower endorsement.

[46] According to MARAD, actively sailing mariners are those who have a record in their sea-service table—a record that they have sailed internationally—within the last 18 months.

[47] *A Report to Congress: Impacts of Reductions in Government Impelled Cargo on the U.S. Merchant Marine.*

[48] A discharge certificate verifies that a mariner sailed on a particular voyage. Section 14.307 of title 46 of the Code of Federal Regulations requires oceangoing U.S.-flag vessels to provide discharge certificates records to USCG regarding mariners sailing internationally, upon USCG request. The certificate includes such information as the mariner's citizenship, rate/rank the mariner is serving on the voyage, date and place of shipment, date and place of discharge, name of the vessel, name of the operating company, class of the vessel, and nature of the voyage.

[49] MARAD officials told us that they analyzed USCG data on the qualified mariners and applied certain assumptions to estimate the number of mariners able to support DOD needs and maintain commercial operations. According to MARAD, the assumptions they used include the following: (1) excluded nonunion mariners, (2) excluded mariners sailing in the Great Lakes, and (3) excluded mariners for whom there was no record that they had sailed within the last 18 months. We requested that MARAD provide us with more detailed methodology to explain how it made and quantified each of these assumptions in making its final estimate. MARAD told us it could not provide any more details about its methodology.

[50] Based on the estimated number of mariners MARAD provided as part of their comments to our draft report, the gap could be as high as 1,754 mariners.

[51] For the purposes of this report, a policy option is a course or principle of action that could be taken by the U.S. government.

[52] We categorized stakeholders into (1) maritime industry stakeholders, which are those stakeholders that we interviewed that self-identified as brokers, carriers, freight forwarders, and mariners, and (2) other maritime stakeholders, which are those stakeholders that we interviewed that self-identified as academia, commodities, freight forwarders, nongovernmental organizations (NGO), ports, and trade associations. We further categorized stakeholders that self-identified as freight forwarders as exclusive freight forwarders or implementing partner freight forwarders. For the purposes of this report, an "exclusive freight forwarder" refers to an agent that provides services for a shipper—in this case, either the U.S. government or an implementing partner. Such services include advising on freight costs, among other costs, and preparing and filing the bill of lading and other required documentation. We categorized "exclusive freight forwarder" under "maritime industry stakeholders." An "implementing partner freight forwarder" refers to a shipper that is working in partnership with an "exclusive freight forwarder," which we categorized under "other maritime stakeholders."

[53] The frequently selected options are those options that were selected by 4 or more stakeholders overall or 3 or more maritime industry stakeholders or other maritime stakeholders. No options were selected as being in the top 3 by more than 4 of the stakeholders.

[54] Each of these options was selected by 4 stakeholders overall, and therefore they are not listed in any particular order.

[55] Each of these options was selected by 3 maritime industry stakeholders, and therefore they are not listed in any particular order.

[56] Each of these options was selected by 3 other maritime stakeholders, and therefore they are not listed in any particular order.

[57] See 7 U.S.C. § 1736o(f)(3).

[58] A rule means the whole or a part of an agency statement of general or particular applicability and future effect designed to implement, interpret, or prescribe law or policy. In this case, according to DOT, as of June 2015, MARAD's proposed rulemaking is in interagency review. MARAD previously advanced proposed rulemakings, which were not successfully promulgated.

[59] According to DOT, certain segments of the U.S.-flag merchant marine have limited vessel capacity, such as dry-bulk and tankers capable of handling small parcels less than 10,000 tons. These are typically full vessel loads subject to the fair and reasonable guideline

process providing USDA and USAID protection from monopolistic-type pricing practices. MARAD has indicated these segments have excess capacity and vessels are often in a lay-up status because of a lack of cargo. It is unlikely new participants would enter these trades with a waiver of the 3-year waiting period provision.

[60] GAO found in 2011 that DOT had no record of an ocean transportation contract awarded to a U.S.-flag vessel that reflagged into the U.S. registry and waited the 3 years prior to applying for food aid contracts; see GAO-11-636. However, according to MARAD, a vessel is currently in the 3-year waiting period and other vessels may have reflagged as U.S.-flag vessels under the 3-year waiting period provision, but this information is not readily available.

[61] Our report will examine only the oceangoing portion of the U.S.-flag fleet that would include vessels that transport food aid internationally. Our report does not focus on vessels that are subject to the Jones Act, a U.S. law that applies to cargo shipped by waterborne transportation between two U.S. points.

[62] Our report focuses on the ocean transportation of commodities procured and shipped for three U.S. international food aid programs: Title II Food for Peace, Food for Progress, and McGovern-Dole International Food for Education and Child Nutrition.

[63] Bulk commodities, such as free-flowing grain and vegetable oil, are those directly loaded and shipped in an ocean vessel's cargo hold. Packaged commodities are those shipped in woven polypropylene bags, multiwalled paper bags, plastic containers, or steel cans and drums. We obtained bid data to ship all USDA food aid and USAID's packaged food aid. We did not include bid data to ship USAID's bulk food aid because these data were not available in the database USDA provided, which was implemented in April 2011. USAID's data of awarded bids (award data) show that bulk commodities accounted for about 50 percent of USAID total commodities in the past few years. However, we did include USAID's bulk commodities in our analysis of all USAID's and USDA's award data.

[64] For the purposes of this report, we use the term "implementing partners" as entities such as NGOs that are awarded U.S. government grants to carry out food assistance activities overseas, and international humanitarian aid organizations. NGOs include international humanitarian aid organizations; international and local private voluntary organizations; and other entities.

[65] We further categorized stakeholders that self-identified as freight forwarders as exclusive freight forwarders or implementing partner freight forwarders. For the purposes of this report, an "exclusive freight forwarder" refers to an agent that provides services for a shipper—in this case, either the U.S. government or an implementing partner. Such services include advising on freight costs, among other costs, and preparing and filing the bill of lading and other required documentation. We categorized "exclusive freight forwarder" under "maritime industry stakeholders." An "implementing partner freight forwarder" refers to a shipper that is working in partnership with an "exclusive freight forwarder," which we categorized under "other maritime stakeholders."

[66] For the purposes of this report, a policy option is a course or principle of action that could be taken by the U.S. government.

[67] We followed up with all 29 stakeholders, but 2 (both other maritime stakeholders) did not prefer any of the suggested options and 9 (6 maritime industry stakeholders and 3 other maritime stakeholders) declined to comment further or did not provide a response after contacting them multiple times. For example, 2 of the 9 stakeholders declined to comment further because their organizations' leadership advised them not to do so.

[68] According to officials from USDA's Kansas City Commodity Office (KCCO), KCCO implemented the changes in the CPFA requirements for solicitations after July 6, 2012.

[69] For USDA's food aid and USAID's packaged food aid, USDA's KCCO applies linear programming software and determines the successful bids by minimizing both commodity and ocean freight costs for the solicitation. The lowest-priced ocean freight bid may not necessarily be awarded the contract.

[70] Pub. L. No. 104-239, § 17. This provision of law was repealed by Section 100124 of Division F of the Moving Ahead for Progress in the 21st Century Act. For the 2010 study, see Elizabeth R. Bageant, Christopher B. Barrett, and Erin C. Lentz, "Food Aid and Agricultural Cargo Preference," *Applied Economic Perspectives and Policy*, 32.4 (2010): 624-641.

[71] The data included four solicitations lines of bulk food aid for USAID which we removed from the analysis. According to KCCO officials, USAID submitted bids for bulk food aid via WBSCM initially but stopped using WBSCM after a few months.

[72] USAID stated that WBSCM's process was not compatible with USAID's process. For example, USAID informed USDA that WBSCM could not account for key information—such as current market conditions, available funding, alternate foreign ports, and available ships with sufficient cargo space. See GAO, *International Food Aid: Better Agency Collaboration Needed to Assess and Improve Emergency Food Aid Procurement System*, GAO-14-22 (Washington, D.C.: Mar. 26, 2014).

[73] Within solicitations, all bids were submitted within 7 days of one another.

[74] The percentage of solicitation lines with matches between the data on bids and shipping awards was higher after the changes in the CPFA requirements (74 percent) than before the changes (69 percent). The difference in these percentages was statistically significant at the 95 percent level. Nonetheless, we found similar results using the data on shipping awards for our analysis on the number of ocean freight bids.

[75] The data on bids do not distinguish between USDA and USAID, and therefore we could not exclude solicitations lines for USAID bulk food aid from this analysis. However, we found four solicitations lines for USAID bulk food aid in the data on awards. Since the data on bids include the solicitation lines in the data on awards, the data on bids include at least four solicitation lines for USAID bulk food aid.

[76] These results were similar when using only the data on awards. The data on awards constitute a subset of the data on bids and represent 72 percent of the solicitation lines in the data on bids.

[77] In other sensitivity analyses, we removed the solicitation lines in the top and bottom 1 percent of shipping rates and the results changed only slightly. This suggests that our results were not driven by solicitation lines with extreme number of bids.

[78] We calculated the simple average over all the solicitation lines before and after the changes in the CPFA requirements.

[79] The shipping rates presented here differ from those presented earlier in the report because these shipping rates are calculated from a different data set that does not include USAID's bulk food aid.

[80] We used the natural logarithm of the shipping rate because it is roughly normally distributed, whereas shipping rates have a distribution that is skewed to the right. For the shipping rate of packaged food aid, we used the gross shipping rate, which includes the cost of shipping the bags containing the food aid. According to USAID officials, it pays the carriers based on the gross shipping rate. Our results are almost identical when excluding the cost of shipping the bags containing the food aid.

[81] We converted the coefficients from table 7 into percentages by taking the exponential of the coefficient, subtracting by 1, and multiplying by 100.

[82] The decrease in shipping rates for USDA was not statistically significant.

[83] The change in the overall shipping rate includes both the changes in the shipping rates on U.S.- and foreign-flag vessels and the increased use of foreign-flag vessels after the changes in the CPFA requirements. In addition, we estimate separate OLS regressions for the overall shipping rate, the shipping rate on U.S.-flag vessels, and the shipping rate on foreign-flag vessels. We estimated these regressions on different-sized samples. Therefore, the change in the overall shipping rate is not a weighted average of the change in shipping rates on U.S.- and foreign-flag vessels.

[84] We converted the coefficients from table 8 into percentages by taking the exponential of the coefficient, subtracting by 1, and multiplying by 100.

[85] In other sensitivity analyses, we removed the solicitation lines in the top and bottom 1 percent of shipping rates and the results changed only slightly. This suggests that our results were not driven by solicitation lines with extreme shipping rates. We also controlled for the total amount of USAID packaged food aid and USDA food aid in the solicitation each month and the results changed slightly. This suggests that our results may not all be driven by the declining amount of food aid.

[86] During our semistructured interviews, we orally explained to stakeholders that our review is focused only on the oceangoing vessels of the U.S.-flag fleet and our review is on the topic of cargo preference for food aid.

INDEX

A

B

C

D

E

F

G

H

I

J

K

L

M

N

O

P

Q

R

S

T

U

V

W